A PLUM IN YOUR MOUTH

A PLUM IN YOUR MOUTH

Why the Way We talk Speaks Volumes About Us

Andrew Taylor

Foreword by Rory Bremner

CHIVERS

British Library Cataloguing in Publication Data available

This Large Print edition published by BBC Audiobooks Ltd, Bath, 2007.
Published by arrangement with HarperCollins Publishers

U.K. Hardcover ISBN 978 1 405 64012 1
U.K. Softcover ISBN 978 1 405 64013 8

Printed and bound in Great Britain by
Antony Rowe Ltd., Chippenham, Wiltshire

For Sam, Abi and Bec

. . . just words, that's all . . .

CONTENTS

FOREWORD

by **Rory Bremner**

Man A: Try pronouncing the word 'a-i-r'.
Man B: Air.
Man A: Good. Now try pronouncing the word 'h-a-i-r'.
Man B: Hair.
Man A: Excellent. Now try the word 'l-a-i-r'.
Man B: Lair.
Man A: Splendid. Now put them together and what have you got?
Man B: Air, hair, lair.
Man A: Welcome to Sandhurst.

I'm fascinated by pronunciation. After all, the fact that there are so many regional and social variations in the way people speak is meat and drink to any impressionist. In an increasingly bland political landscape, where it's hard to tell the Hoon from the what, the distinctive accent and vowel sounds of a Prescott, a Gordon Brown or, God help us, an Ian Paisley, are manna from Heaven.

I'm delighted, therefore, that someone has at last undertaken the daunting task of making a proper study of the whole subject of pronunciation. (Or should that be *proNOUNciation*?). And not just contemporary pronunciation, either: here you will find a wealth of fascinating historical detail about how the way we speak has altered over the years and from region to region.

For my own part, I don't analyse accents in any particularly rigorous way. Mimicry is instinctive, the product of a musical ear that recognises and likes to imitate the different sounds and cadences of another's voice. From an early age, my mother devoted hours to my music practice. It was only later that she confessed to being tone deaf, so I could have been playing anything. In the event, my instinct to imitate was so strong that before long I was just copying the teacher and playing by ear, with the result that I soon lost the ability to read music.

Because it's instinctive, it's very difficult to break down how I identify and reproduce the particular characteristics that distinguish one voice from another. I generally start with what *kind* of voice I'm trying to copy. Is it a very breathy sort of voice like Ian McCaskill's or very deep like Gordon Brown; nasal like Antony Worrall Thompson, adenoidal like Melvyn Bragg or open and sibilant like to Tony Blair's? Only then can I concentrate on the words, and in particular the vowel sounds, from the long, open Geordie vowels of Ant and Dec, (*Are ye gauwing owaya?*) to the distinctive *o*'s of a Malcolm Rifkind or a David Steel. Impressionists sometimes construct whole sentences around a particular vowel, rather like using the phrase *hi nigh, brine kye* to illustrate a Northern Irish accent. For the former Liberal leader, David Steel, I would begin with the nonsense phrase 'I would certainly hoe-p that I could coe-p with enough roe-p to hang myself,' purely to locate his accent. For Malcolm Rifkind, I adapted the song 'Moses supposes his toeses are roses' to apply to policy regarding Saddam Hussein ('That presupposes he knows we oppose his proposals') purely to enjoy his uniquely fruity *o* sounds. John Major talks about *Streeeowd Teeown Ceeowncil.* With Michael Howard, it was his idiosyncratic way of pronouncing the letter *l.* He only had to talk of *schooools* or *hospitalllls* to reduce the House of Commons to hoots of laughter and derisive mimicry.

There may be dropped consonants as well, either genuine or affected, as in the case of Tony Blair when he's trying to sound like a man of the people (you've always got to remember that he's an actor before anything else). Hence, 'We've go' a' think abou' i',' where the *t* is silent. He's even flattened the *it* sound at the end of *benefit* to produce the word *benefeh.* You can hear him at the Despatch Box at *Prime Minister's Questions*, desperately trying not to sound like a Fettes schoolboy: 'Ah tell yer.' Then there's a bizarre noise he uses in the Commons, a bit like a triumphal sneer, when he thinks he's on to

xi

something the opposition don't want to hear but he's going to repeat anyway. It doesn't seem to have any vowels or consonants at all—something like *er-ayar!*—which he repeats three or four times. I think it probably started off as *oh, yes,* but you can't be sure. But he retains some interesting Scottish pronunciation: like his old flatmate Lord Falconer (and Ronnie Corbett), he says *inshoo-er* for *ensure*—that's very Edinburgh—which goes to show you can't completely escape the accents of your peers.

It's a particular British trait that we use pronunciation and accent to locate someone's geographical and social background. (See 'Air, hair, lair' above.) A striking example is the letter *r*: there's a *ve'y ve'y* upper class habit of dropping the *r* in the middle of a word.

Station and continuity announcements used to have to be very clipped Received Pronunciation, so much so that they now sound extraordinarily dated and paternalistic, and are perceived as snobbish and elitist. Today, the tendency has gone the other way; it's not uncommon to be greeted by a prerecorded telephone message that is so heavily accented and informal, in an attempt to cosy up to the caller, that I, for one, resent the implied 'mateyness'.

Unusual pronunciation can also have unintended comic effects. I've often wondered why George W. Bush is so taken with the word 'merkin', meaning 'pubic wig'. Yet he uses it in many of his speeches: 'Ah'm proud to be a merkin.' When I was at school, we all had to fill in university application forms called UCCA forms—UCCA pronounced *Ucker*. My friend Simon Cox's father almost fell off his chair when a housemaster rang up and asked, 'Where's the Cox UCCA?' Sean Connery has a distinctive *sh* sound when he says an *s*. We were standing around at a barbecue once when he suddenly asked, 'Why aren't we shitting?' I thought, 'Well, because you haven't eaten my barbecue yet.' It was only when he added the qualification, 'Why aren't we shitting down' that I understood what he meant.

By and large though, I don't share the class snobbery about accents. For me, they are a reflection of a rich variety of influences, classes and cultures that make up the United Kingdom and distinguish us as individuals. And without them I'd be lost. Fortunately, people are generally flattered to be mimicked. Like they say, 'You're nobody till somebody does you.'

So I'm pleased to welcome a book devoted to the way we speak. Fellow enthusiasts browsing the bookshelves will pronounce it a sight for sore eyes. Unless, of course, they happen to be Sean Connery.

INTRODUCTION

Danny the Red and the Deadly Tomato

More serious-minded people might remember Laurence Olivier in *Hamlet*, or possibly a recording of Winston Churchill's wartime speeches, and they might have written a different book. But I remember little, round, Danny the Red.

He was a young French assistant at my grammar school in the 1960s, and we called him Danny the Red after the leader of the rioting French students because he had once told us proudly that he was a communist—but he certainly had no egalitarian or internationalist ideas where we were concerned. He was filled with Gallic pride and high seriousness, and had a strict frown and a very expressive curl of the lip to show his disdain for the English in general and us in particular. He also had a very highly developed sense of what was proper and decent. He was only about five feet two, but that wasn't why we took advantage of him so mercilessly. After all, Napoleon was not much bigger than that, and he conquered most of Europe.

No, it was his French accent.

One day, he announced that he was setting us a written test and rapped sternly on the

1

desk to demand our attention. In front of him was an intimidating pile of blank paper. 'I am going to give each of you a piss of pepper!' he declared, and the class collapsed in fits of giggles. Well, we *were* only 15.

Danny looked around, his mounting anger only matched by his puzzlement. 'I don' see why it is fonny to 'ave a piss of pepper,' he shouted above the din, spitting out his *p*'s in fury. 'OK, so I don' give you a piss of pepper. I give you a *shit* of pepper!'

Not a piece but a *piss*. Not a sheet but a *shit*. As I howled with laughter, along with the rest of the class of grubby-minded adolescents, the tiniest inkling of the immense and random power of the spoken word was sown in my chimpanzee-like immature brain. There was nothing remarkable about the words he'd *said*, but the words we'd *heard* were completely different.

*   *   *

I don't feel too guilty about the way we treated Danny—people have been making fun of unfamiliar accents for as long as humans have been rude to each other. The dismissive word *barbarian* comes originally from an ancient Sanskrit word referring to the unintelligible *bar, bar, bar* sound with which foreigners seemed to speak, so they were certainly at it six or seven thousand years ago.

But it all depends on where you are standing. In London, an Englishman who pronounced his *r*'s in words like *farmer* or *car park* might be sniggered at behind his back as a rustic buffoon, but in most of the United States, anyone who *didn't* pronounce his *r*'s would sound like an oik. *R*-dropping there loses as many social brownie points as *h*-dropping does in Britain. The point of the joke, whether it is a Sanskrit scribe thousands of years ago writing about the way foreigners speak or a comedian today doing his mock-Pakistani accent in some Working Men's club, is always the same. They don't sound like us, so they aren't like us: it's all about belonging.

But even though it's a joke that has been passed around throughout history, it has a very limited currency. An Old Etonian banker in the City might poke fun at the flat *a*'s and rounded *u*'s of a northern colleague, or they might both snigger at the long *r* sounds of a Westcountryman, but if they suggested to an American how odd the accents sounded, they would be met with a blank stare. All the American would hear would be three English voices with not a lot to tell them apart.

The joke can sometimes be very black indeed. During Lebanon's civil wars in the 1980s, armed gangs would drag people from cars at illegal checkpoints and hold up a tomato. 'What is that?' they would ask, as if it were a children's game. Palestinians would say

'Bandura' and Lebanese 'Banadura'. But no one was laughing. It was a bloodthirsty version of 'You say tomayto and I say tomahto': get the wrong one and you were out of the game for good, shot dead at the side of the road. There were similar stories about gunmen during The Troubles in Northern Ireland, who would ask people the name of the high-street jeweller H. Samuel—Protestants would say 'aitch' and Catholics 'haitch', with the same savage result. During the Second World War, during the civil wars in the former Yugoslavia, on the streets of Iraq, during practically every ethnic, national or racial conflict, the same brutal method has been used to tell friend from foe. Differences over pronunciation can be, quite literally, deadly serious.

Those are extreme examples. Most anxieties over pronunciation today are not about getting shot, but about not being accepted—anxieties about what your voice says about you. Christine Keeler, the woman at the centre of the Profumo scandal that nearly brought down a government in the 1960s, objected bitterly to being described as a 'scrubber' in a ghost-written autobiography published under her name some years later. It wasn't the suggestion of sexual immorality that angered her—the papers had been filled with lurid stories about the British Minister for War and the Russian Defence Attaché bouncing by turn in and out of her warm and welcoming bed. It was what

4

she took as the implication that she didn't speak properly. In a very English way, it was her behaviour in the drawing-room, not the bedroom, that she wanted to defend: 'I wanted them to change it to "tart". Scrubber implies someone who can't talk properly and wears horrible clothes, but I always spoke well, and had good clothes,' she said.[1] She was happy enough, in other words, for people to suggest that she dropped her knickers, but not that she dropped her aitches.

More recently,[2] Sir Charles Ronald George Nall-Cain—Lord Brocket for short—told a television audience that it was always easy to recognize a real aristocrat. 'It's partly a question of character and values,' beamed this convicted fraudster who spent two and a half years as Her Majesty's guest in seven different prisons. 'But the obvious clue,' he added, with a snickering laugh, 'is if you've got a toff's accent like mine!'

He was mistaken, of course. The old days when a cut-glass accent was a passport to social respectability are long gone, and today, people are more likely to put their effort into losing a privileged accent than into acquiring one. Tony Blair has cultivated his glottal stops and abandoned his Fettes accent with as much care as Harold Wilson tended his Yorkshire vowels nearly half a century ago. But it's the rules that have changed, not the game itself, and people with an unfashionably broad regional accent may still find themselves struggling in interviews for jobs or university places. There are clear advantages to speaking in a way that sticks fairly closely to one or other of a few 'acceptable' models.

For all the different accents though, we all sound pretty similar—up to a point. We can immediately tell any sort of English from, say, French, by the *th* and *h* sounds, which don't appear in French, or by the distinctive back-of-the-throat *r* sound which does. We could tell it from Russian because of the different rhythm of the sentences, or from Chinese by the unfamiliar tones. But though all the accents of English use a recognizably similar set of distinctive sounds, they use them in different ways. From hearing a single sentence, most people can say with a fair degree of accuracy whether a speaker comes from America, Australia, Scotland or Cornwall.

There are changes not just over distance but over time as well. In the opening scenes of Hitchcock's famous film *Rebecca*, Mrs Edythe Van Hopper invites the unwilling Max de Winter to join her in the hotel lobby. 'Coffeh? Esk thet stupid waitah for enether cep!' In 1940, those strangled vowels were fashionable and distinguished: today, they just sound as if they've been rescued from the back shelf of a museum. That's a minor change over a few decades, but the story of English stretches back over a thousand years and includes different tribes and different nationalities who might hardly ever speak to each other. It's not surprising that different ways of pronouncing the language should have developed among the various communities that were scattered over the country.

So dialects and regional accents grew up. But the vast majority of people today, far from recognizing accents with any precision, aren't even aware of how they speak themselves. If you ask someone whether they pronounce the word *plastic* with a flat *a* or a rounded *a*, for instance, or whether they sound the *t* in the word *often*, they will usually try the alternatives out a couple of times before deciding how to answer. And if you listen to them speaking when they are not thinking about it, they will frequently pronounce the words quite differently anyway. We all say words in one way when we read them out in a list, in a different way when they crop up in a sentence in a book, and in yet another when we use them in conversation. Most people who were brought up with any sort of regional accent can slip in and out of it almost without a thought.

The point of this book is to make us more aware of how we sound. It's not a guide to 'correct' pronunciation—if there is such a thing—and it's certainly not intended as a scholarly study of linguistics or phonology. You will search in vain for any mention of bilabial plosives, fricatives, or laterals, [Well, all right.

7

A bilabial plosive is the explosive release of air between the two lips. A fricative occurs when air is expelled between the lips or between the lip and the tongue with such force that the friction between them is audible, and a lateral is a sound which is made by allowing the air to escape around the sides of the tongue. By great good fortune, you can remember bilabial plosives as b's and p's, fricatives as f's (or z, h, s or sh), and laterals as l's. But that is the last time they will be mentioned.] and there will be none of the symbols of the International Phonetic Alphabet. I am concerned with why we speak as we do, and what effect it has on us. Is it true, as George Bernard Shaw famously said, that 'it is impossible for an Englishman to open his mouth without making some other Englishman despise him'[3]—and if it is, then does it have to be?

So this book is not another nit-picking, fault-finding grumble about the way people are mangling our beautiful language: rather, it is a celebration of the greatest single achievement of the human race. Without the development of language hundreds of thousands of years ago—and by the word language, until people started writing things down about three or four thousand years ago, we mean exclusively *spoken* language—none of the other discoveries which led to the growth of civilization would have been possible. Fire, the use of tools, and the wheel would all have been no more than occasional amusements if their inventors had lacked the ability to pass on their ideas. It was speech that set humanity free.

On a simple physical level, speaking is an astonishing achievement. The tiny and infinitely subtle movements of the muscles of the chest, the larynx and the mouth, the degree of force with which air is blown between lips that are held in exactly the correct formation, and the delicate positioning of the tongue all have to be precisely right to produce the sounds that we recognize. Practically everyone can do it—and yet practically no one realizes exactly what they are doing. How many people could list in detail the different movements involved in speaking the simplest sentence?

But it goes beyond that. The control of pitch, intonation, and volume enables us to pass on the tiniest shades of meaning. We can make the single, virtually meaningless word 'Oh' express surprise, joy, disappointment, anger, despair, happiness, wonder, boredom, delight, grief, amazement, sympathy, longing, regret, pain, or dawning comprehension, entirely by the way that we say it. Write down the sentence *The cup is quite full* and no one will know what you mean: say it, and put a slight stress on the word *full*, and you mean it's brimming over. Put the stress on the word *quite* and you mean exactly the opposite. It's *quite* full, but not quite *full*. Again, virtually no one could explain exactly *how* they do it, but everyone *can* do it without a thought. Language belongs to all of us, not just to the experts.

That doesn't mean, of course, that the way we speak isn't important. It's not just what we say that reveals who we are, but the way that we say it. And why does that matter? Remember the tomato—*bandura* or *banadura*? Are you with us or against us?

CHAPTER ONE

Talking Proper

Received Pronunciation—why posh people talk the way they do

There must *be* rules about language or nobody would ever understand anybody else. Elocution teachers and voice coaches make a good living out of teaching people how to improve the way they speak; people write to the newspapers and ring up the BBC to complain when they think they've heard a mispronunciation, and we've all felt that stab of irritation when a well-meaning friend informs us that it's *sliver* to rhyme with *river*, not *sliver* to rhyme with *diver*, or *paytronize* with a long *a*, not *patronize* with a short one— so there must be a standard somewhere by which we can all be judged. (With those two last examples, the *Longman Pronunciation Dictionary*, the closest thing we have to an authoritative standard for the modern pronunciation of English words, tells us that both versions are in common use. So there.) The trouble is, leaving aside the *LPD*, which claims to describe how words *are* pronounced, not how they *should* be, it's very difficult to decide what the standard is.

We all want to be understood, of course—

but there's more to it than that. English is spoken in hundreds of different accents, but some of them will make people's hackles rise and others will make waiters fawn like cringing puppies. Defining which is which is not easy: two examples will probably do the job best.

The judge was very grand, with pretensions to be even grander, and he was sitting in London's Snaresbrook Crown Court, which is where the seedier of the criminal cases involving East End villains tend to end up. Prosecuting counsel was describing a case of burglary in Hertfordshire, when the judge stopped him, looking down from the bench with a long, reproving stare. The lawyer had committed a serious crime.

'Those of us who live in the county,' which he pronounced *kinety*, 'refah to it as *Har'f'dshee-ah*,' the judge intoned solemnly, with a definitive stress on the final word. Nobody smiled, and prosecuting counsel nodded repentantly, eyes on his desk so as not to meet the gaze of the great man, and continued with his opening address. The defendant, he told the judge, came from the London borough of Hackney—and, unprompted, the defendant leaned forward helpfully in the dock, and said, 'Vose of us wot lives vere caws it 'Eckney.'

It's not known whether he paid any price later in the case for his helpfulness, but between them, the judge, the barrister and the criminal had just produced a strikingly theatrical definition of the difference between prestigious and stigmatized accents.

The second example came in a recent letter to *The Times*. In December 2005, the British prime minister committed an apparently unforgivable crime against humanity. Greeting the newly-elected German chancellor, Angela Merkel, Tony Blair shook her hand, *keeping his own left hand in his jacket pocket*. The letter-writer expressed the outrage of a shocked and humiliated nation. 'Even men who speak Estuary English naturally, and not for political purposes, generally know how to treat a lady,' he said. Leaving aside the writer's disproportionate shame at Blair's apparent lack of *savoir faire*, and the slightly clodhopping political irony that suggests that the prime minister spends time carefully honing his accent in front of an elocution teacher, the message is clear: *even* men who speak Estuary English—the casual, easy-going London style of speech which we will look at in detail in a later chapter—know how to behave. Like the defendant's broad Cockney, that too, at least according to *The Times* letters page, says something vaguely discreditable about people who use it.

Patronizing (or *paytronizing*) or what? That letter, together with the judge's self-satisfied pomposity, goes a long way towards explaining George Bernard Shaw's point. He was, of course, was indulging in the Irish national sport of winding up the English—and for Englishmen who want to get into an argument, it's worth remembering what Dr Johnson once said about another pontificating Irishman: 'What entitles Sheridan to fix the pronunciation of English?' the old bear growled. 'He has in the first place the disadvantage of being an Irishman.' But Shaw had a point—so why do the English despise each other so readily? Regional accents may reveal where a person comes from, but few people would think that was any reason for contempt. It's only among football hooligans and psychopaths that people inspire hatred and derision simply by being born in the wrong place, so the fact that Geordies talk differently from Welshmen, that people from Norfolk have different vowel sounds from people in the West Country, or that Australians and Americans don't sound the same offers no explanation.

We may find an unfamiliar accent odd or even funny, or we may even struggle to understand it; there is no obvious reason why we should write it off as contemptible. But of course, the way we speak says more about us than just where we were born: it helps to fix our standing in society. It's hard, for instance, even in the relatively socially mobile world of the twenty-first century, to imagine the accents of judge and criminal being reversed. People expect the way we speak to reveal who we are.

Or rather, they expect it to slot us into one of a series of preconceptions. A thick Yorkshire accent, for instance, would suggest someone was a bit slow and unimaginative; a West Country voice could clearly only come from a simple and unsophisticated country bumpkin; and—certainly in Snaresbrook Crown Court—anyone who speaks broad Cockney could only be in the dock or, at a pinch, the witness box. It is, of course, all 'bunkum and balderdash' as Sir Bernard Ingham, Lady Thatcher's former Downing Street press officer, used to say in his gruff Yorkshire accent. Not many people would have called him 'slow' (or at least, not twice); and 'unimaginative' would have been the last word to apply to the late Ted Hughes, Poet Laureate and one of the leading poets of the twentieth century, who spoke all his life with the accent of his native Mytholmroyd, in West Yorkshire's Brontë country.

Colin Pillinger, Professor of Planetary Sciences at the Open University, PhD, DSc, and a whole alphabet soup of other qualifications and honours, not to mention Fellow of the Royal Society, Fellow of the Royal Astronomical Society, and the man behind the 2004 Beagle II Mars probe, would not be everyone's idea of a country bumpkin, despite his thick Bristol accent. And it would be a surprise to find Janet Street-Porter, for instance, or the film star Terence Stamp, Cockney voices and all, in the dock at Snaresbrook or anywhere else.

So if we know as soon as we think about it that the prejudices are nonsense, then where do they come from? They have certainly been around for a long time. There have always been people who want to disguise their origins and others, generally higher up the social scale, who want to show how different they are from everybody else. Language is one of the main tools that they both use—but if we want someone to blame for our obsession with accents, we could start with William Caxton, who produced Britain's first printed book in 1477. Until then, none of the patchwork of different regional dialects and accents across England had been considered better or more desirable than the others.

The reason was simple: William the Conqueror had brought his own language with him from Normandy in 1066, and for more than 200 years, Norman French, not English, was the language of the court and the upper classes. The old English aristocracy had been virtually wiped out in the years that followed the Conquest: there was no formal standard of the speech or language of a defeated people.

Caxton's books were instrumental in changing that, although he himself rejected any suggestion that he was the person to set standards for grammar, vocabulary, or speech.

Like everyone else, he spoke in a local dialect: 'I . . . was born and lerned myn Englissh in Kente in the Weeld, where I doubte not is spoken as brode and rude Englissh as is in ony place of Englond,' he declared. In *Troilus and Criseyde*—one of Caxton's first books—the poet Geoffrey Chaucer wondered how far across England his work would be understood, 'for ther is so gret diversite/In Englissh and in writing of oure tonge'.

But he needn't have worried: London was already by far the richest and most powerful city in England, and the language which Caxton set in type was Chaucer's own, essentially that of London and the south-east. That was where his books were printed and most of their readers were to be found, and it was their version of the language that was literally set out in black and white on his pages. Over the following decades, it became accepted as the standard way of writing English. Then as now, the attitude was that if it was written down, then it must be right— once the way of writing the language in the south-east of England had been accepted as a standard, it was only a matter of time before the way of speaking it would follow.

Regional accents survived, of course: one of the people who read the *Canterbury Tales* was Richard, Duke of Gloucester—brought up in Wensleydale, Yorkshire—who brought his northern voice and his northern friends to

London when he seized the crown as King Richard III. Think of Prince Charles speaking like Geoffrey Boycott. A hundred years later in the late 1580s, when William Shakespeare arrived in London he would almost certainly have spoken with a broad Warwickshire accent, saying *woonder* for *wonder*, *smoake* for *smoke*, and *daunger* for *danger*. He would have rolled his *r*'s and lengthened the final syllable of words like *legacy* or *perjury*.

At the beginning of the seventeenth century, the Catholic publisher and antiquary Richard Verstegan described the different ways that people spoke in different parts of the country. 'One would say at London, "I would eat more cheese yf I had it",' he said. 'The northern man saith, "Ay sud eat mare cheese gin ay hadet", and the westerne man saith, "Chud eat more cheese an chad it".' There were even rustic tones to be heard at court: the urbane and sophisticated Sir Walter Raleigh was known for his broad Devonshire vowels, although the fact that people talked about it suggests that this was unusual. The establishment of a single prestigious version of the language meant that 'country speech' would always be seen as an inferior way of talking.

And it was not only the country bumpkins who were to be looked down on: gentlemen, it seemed, should look to their own households, and beware of the corrupting feminine influence on their children. Writing in 1531, Sir Thomas Elyot declared that they should choose as teachers only those who 'speke none englisshe but that which is clene, polite, perfectly and articulately pronounced, omitting no letter or syllable as foolish women oftentimes do of a wantonesse, whereby divers noble men and gentilmennes children . . . have attained corrupte and foule pronunciation.' So it was the women who were to blame!

But how do we know how people spoke hundreds of years ago? The past, after all, is silent, or at least it was until Edison invented the phonograph. No-one speaks to us from there. We can read the words people wrote but we can't hear how they said them. All we have is guesswork based on scanty evidence—and it's the experts who think they know most who are the least help. When scholars try to describe pronunciation in writing, it can be meaningless to later readers. In 1547, William Salesbury, the leading Welsh scholar of the Renaissance, produced his *Dictionary in Englyshe and Welshe* and included what was intended as a helpful note on how the Welsh language of his day should be pronounced. The letter *u*, he said, 'soundeth as the vulgar English people sound it in these wordes of English: *trust*, *bury*, *busy*,' which might have been some guide in 1547 but tells us precious little now—not least, of course, because today most people would pronounce the vowels in

19

his three words quite differently from each other—*trust*, *berry* and *bizzy*.

The grumblers—writers who complain about the standard of spoken English in their own day—have a bit more to say. In the eighteenth century they were, if anything, even more bitter than they are today. Linguistic scholars at the time were keen to show that the 'proper' pronunciation of a word was fixed by its spelling—but in describing the way it ought to be pronounced, they had also to describe as best they could how people actually spoke it. Isaac Watts, a non-conformist minister in London who also considered himself qualified to lay down the law about how people should speak, included *coff* for *cough* and *mets'n* for *medicine* in a list of pronunciations that were common in London, 'especially among the vulgar'. But the pronunciations they hated are the ones that survived: the fact that the scholars lost and the ordinary people—the 'vulgar'—won is a useful reminder of how futile it is to tell people how to speak.

The biggest changes in pronunciation came during the Middle Ages, after Chaucer died. William Shakespeare was born around the end of the process, which means that the language of his plays is generally at least recognizable today, but Chaucer, at the end of the fourteenth century, might almost be writing in a foreign language. Within the first four lines of *The Canterbury Tales*, he throws a rhyme at us which goes straight past a modern audience:

April showers have ended the drought of March
And bathed every veyne in swich licour
Of which vertu engendred is the flour . . .

Licour is the fourteenth-century equivalent of the modern word *liquor*, which during 700 years has lost not only its final *r* sound in British English but also the long vowel which produced the final *oor*. The word is now pronounced *lick-uh*, while *flour* (*flower*) has split into two separate syllables—*flow-uh*, not *floo-r*. What was a good rhyme for Chaucer is no rhyme at all for us. Evidence like this, built up and supported from scores of different sources, helps to show how English has changed over the centuries.

By Elizabethan times, despite Raleigh's example, if you wanted to be taken seriously as a gentleman, you had to talk like one. In 1589, the Elizabethan country landowner George Puttenham offered his advice: 'Take the vsuall speach of the Court, and that of London and the shires lying about London within sixty myles, and not much aboue. I say not this but that in euery shyre of England there be gentlemen and others that speake but specially write as good Southerne as we of Middlesex or Surrey do . . .' So by the time of Shakespeare, what had been one dialect among many had become the form of speech to which ambitious people would aspire. Englishmen had started to despise each other's way of speaking.

* * *

The explanation for Shaw's comment was class. As simple as that. It goes back a long way: Evelyn Waugh tells a story in his diaries about his outrage at Lancing public school in 1919, when he and his colleagues in the cadet force were inspected by an officer who was 'the most blatantly risen-from-the-ranks I've ever seen.'[4] The officer in question had just returned from the trenches, where he had been to fight in the war to end all wars, but that mattered nothing compared to the scandal of a young gentleman like Waugh being inspected by an oik with an accent. Some sixty-five years later, the Conservative MP Julian Critchley bewailed the way his party had been taken over by 'small-town solicitors and estate agents with flat provincial accents.'[5]

Regional accents—provincial accents, in Critchley's dismissive phrase—place us on the map, but they can—or they could—be used to place us in society too. And that is where we come to RP and the way that speech divides us. It is probably significant that the phrase 'Received Pronunciation' sounds slightly dusty and out of date. It has a whiff of 'the done thing' and using the proper knife and fork about it—the same sort of condescending arrogance that marked the publication of 'U and non-U' in the 1950s, with its anxiety over whether we were using serviettes or napkins, and eating lunch or dinner. People used to say that the U phrases were the simple, unpretentious ones, although it seems a bit odd to accept advice about unpretentiousness from anyone who compiles a list of the words that we ought to use. The same applies to RP, which might often just as well stand for Really Pretentious rather than Received Pronunciation—but it continues to hang like a damp fog over the whole subject of how we speak.

What's acceptable changes, of course. Fifty years ago, *yes* was correct and *yeah* was the sort of vulgar Americanism that middle-class fathers clipped their children round the ear for saying. But then, during the 1970s and 1980s, *yeah* gradually transformed itself into *yah*, the Princess Diana *yah*, the Harvey Nicks *yah*, or simply the OK *yah*. Not RP, perhaps, but certainly accepted among the rich and trendy. The Americanism had been picked up, sandpapered down, and polished into Knightsbridge-speak.

It's all subjective. When the British linguistic expert Daniel Jones[6] used the phrase 'Received Pronunciation' in 1918 to describe the most prestigious accent of his day, he admitted that his ideas were 'based on my own (southern) speech'—but he added that this accent was 'that regularly used by those who have been educated at "preparatory" boarding schools and the "public schools".' It never claimed, in other words, to represent the language that was spoken by the vast majority of native English speakers, who generally had more or less marked regional accents. Most modern estimates are that around 3 per cent of speakers could be considered today as speaking RP, and the figure is unlikely to have been any higher in Jones's time.

One quality which everyone could agree on about Received Pronunciation, however, was that it effectively disguised whereabouts a person came from. There had been anxiety in fashionable circles for centuries about the fact that, although written English had been more or less fixed, people were much less biddable about the way they spoke. It was the growth of public schools in the nineteenth century that made it possible to establish an accent that might unite people from the different regions of the country—always assuming, of course, that they were rich enough to go to the schools in question. Instead of speaking with an accent which revealed their geographical background, they began to speak with an accent that revealed their social class. At various times, and for obvious reasons, Received Pronunciation has been referred to as 'Standard English', 'public school English', 'Oxford English', 'BBC English', or, with even greater social ambition, 'the Queen's English'. It is also the accent which most people in England use when they claim to speak without an accent.

But what *is* RP? A generation of Marxist linguistic scholars in the 1970s and 1980s declared that it was just another version of English which had been imposed by people with power and social status—that the toffs, in effect, had hi-jacked the language. The Cambridge don Raymond Williams, for example, described Standard English as 'a selected (class-based) use' which 'attempted to convict a majority of native speakers of English of speaking their own language "incorrectly".'[7] Another academic, the Manchester University professor Tony Crowley, declared that it was 'not a form around which radical struggle was to be focused, though it was promulgated and acknowledged in various cultural modes for specific ends.' I don't think I understand that phrase, but it demonstrates beautifully how academic writing about English can sometimes be a language of its own, just as incomprehensible to non-speakers as some South Seas pidgin.

But RP is more than just another accent of English. It is regional accents, not RP, which are exclusive and stop outsiders from understanding. Imagine an American from the Southern States, an Indian who learned his

English in New Delhi, and a Scotsman with a broad Highland accent all travelling together on the London Underground and trying to have a conversation—they may find it difficult to understand each other, but as they get off the train, none of them will have any trouble with the recorded words 'Stand clear of the doors' or 'Please mind the gap'. The announcements may sound as if they were recorded fifty years ago or more, but anyone who speaks English will know what they mean. RP is the closest thing we have in Britain to an accent that will be understood throughout the English-speaking world. It is also the version of English which most foreigners will try to pick up when they learn the language. Partly because of that, and also because of the influence of international broadcasting, it is the accent which non-Britons would imagine as 'British English'.

Everyone, then, can imagine what RP is—but describing the sounds which constitute it is almost impossible. Like those books of patterns which seem to be no more than abstract swirls when you look at them closely, but which resolve themselves into recognizable images as you draw slowly away from them, the shape and the sound of Received Pronunciation become clearer as you take a broader view. Individual words may have different pronunciations that might be equally acceptable, so that the word *financial*, for example, might be pronounced *finnanshul*, *fine-anshull* or even *f'nanshull*, and nobody would even notice; the same person might use each different pronunciation at various times. When people ride horses, do they talk about *horssiz* or *horssuz*? *Russeeved* is just as received as *risseeved*, and *recconize* just as recognized as *recognize*. And do they say *possibly* or *possubly*?

There are many such examples of words like that, where the differences are not even registered in normal conversations. There are certainly many more of them than there are of words that cause CONtroversy (or possibly conTROversy), such as *KILometre* or *kilOmetre*, *skedule* or *shedule*, *HARass* or *harASS*. Does anyone often distinguish between *off'n* and *off-tun*, or, again, between *agen* and *agayn*? Left to ourselves, without the prod-nosed pedants and the writers of the more tedious letters to the newspapers, we seem to be a pretty tolerant people.

Take a slightly broader focus than individual words, and the outline of RP begins to become clearer. Its *a*'s—or some of them— are rounded, so that *bath* is *barth* and *castle* is *carssel*, but its *u*'s are firmly unrounded, so that the u in *cup* is different from the one in *put*. Its *r*'s in words like *farm*, *cart* or *morning* have vanished. It is easier to define, in fact, in terms of what it is not rather than what it is: not northern, not western, not London. The whole point of RP is its geographical anonymity.

27

There are also, of course, habits that are so widespread across England that they can't be considered as regional accents, but which are still emphatically not RP. Dropped *h*'s at the start of words like *happy* and *ham sandwich*, and dropped *g*'s in *dancin'* and *grumblin'*, not to mention words like *'Eadin'ley* or *'angin'*, where you get two for the price of one, are all unmistakable social markers. It's not simply lazy speech—the laziest Americans, Scotsmen and Geordies never drop their *h*'s, while the most hard-working (or should that be *'ardworkin'*?) Southerners sometimes do. And it's not a simple bone-headed failure to understand the 'rules'—even if someone could explain a reason why *heir* and *honest* should have no *h* sound. They are French words, of course—but then, so are *horrible* and *harmony*. The dropped *g*'s have a logic of their own: they are only dropped on unstressed syllables, so while people may say *'angin'*, they would never say *'an'in'*. There's seldom any confusion between *sing* and *sin*: the non-standard version of the language has its own rules that are every bit as strict as RP.

As for the cardinal sin of the dropped *h*— well, the least you can say for it is that it goes back a long way . . . The original English forms of *horrible*, *habit*, and *harmony* were *orryble*, *abit* and *armonie* at around the fourteenth and fifteenth centuries—it was only pedantic scribes a couple of centuries later who, showing off their knowledge of Latin, brought the *h*'s back. The French, of course, stopped pronouncing the initial *h*'s on words like *horrible* (from *horribilis*) and *homme* (from *homo*) as if they were—er—*'ot* very early on in their adaptation of Latin, along with the final *t* on words like *lait*, and have happily adopted both habits as part of their standard, prestigious speech. In English, pronouncing or not pronouncing our *h*'s has, through the centuries, been simply a matter of fashion: forget about the more embarrassing pastimes that malevolent Frenchmen sometimes suggest are uniquely English pleasures: *h*-dropping is the true English vice.

So, if we are talking about what RP is not, we have to add that it is not some pure form of the language, reaching back to the ancient roots of English. The rounded *a* and the unrounded *u* are, as we will see later, simply modern interlopers dating back no more than a few centuries. RP is a convenience, not the guardian of the language. It has no particular loyalty to the way the language is spelt, either—the *r* that you can hear in the south-west of England, in Scotland or in much of the United States, producing phrases like *starrt the carr*, is much closer to the spelling than the anaemic *staht the cah* of 'correct' RP. But then, whoever said that language was about reason, logic or consistency? RP is what it is because of the survival of some fashions of speech, and the withering away of others; its importance today is simply that it is accepted. Dusty and out-of-date the phrase 'Received Pronunciation' may be, but in the end, it is fairly accurate. However few people actually speak it in their daily lives, and however much the Marxist socio-linguists may complain, RP remains the version of English which is most widely received and understood.

An accent, on the other hand, is generally something that other people have: the most fastidious speaker of RP in Britain, with a determinedly 'accentless' voice, will find as soon as he travels to New York that, as far as the people he talks to are concerned, he has acquired a quaint English accent during his flight. And it's not even necessary to leave Britain.

The novelist Arnold Bennett spoke with broad West Midlands vowels all his life—in a rather wistful reference to one of his characters, he says that he spoke with an accent that 'was less local—there was a hint of a short "e" sound in the "a", and a briskness about the consonants, that Edwin could never have compassed.'[8] His contemporary, Aleister Crowley, traveller, mystic, writer, oddball and self-proclaimed Wickedest Man in the World, observed patronizingly about him in the 1920s that 'his accent and dialect made his English delightfully difficult'—but went on to report that Bennett, promising to introduce him to

30

H. G. Wells, observed patronizingly to *him* that 'there was one thing about Wells that I mustn't mind: he spoke English with an accent.'**9**

As indeed he did—Wells, coming from Bromley in south London, was often teased for sounding like a Cockney. But the story doesn't end there. Crowley himself was the son of a prosperous brewer and a graduate of Trinity College Cambridge, but in another set of contemporary memoirs, Anthony Powell, the author of *A Dance to the Music of Time*, remembers a lunch invitation from him with just as much disdain as he showed to Bennett and as Bennett showed to Wells. 'I had never met him, but his celebrated near-Cockney accent grated at once on the ear, as familiar from stories,' he wrote.**10**

Since Powell's background was Eton and Oxford, it's fairly safe to assume what *his* accent would have been—so he was sneering at Crowley, who was sneering at Bennett, who was sneering at H. G. Wells. It's like the famous comedy sketch where Ronnie Barker looks *up* to John Cleese because he's upper class, but *down* to Ronnie Corbett because he is working class: four distinguished literary figures, each showing the same lofty condescension towards the others' way of speaking.

RP was born in the public schools, and it is still widely seen as an indicator of how

31

educated a person may be—with the effect that when individuals fail to meet the standards that are set for them, it can spark real anger. The *Daily Telegraph* cricket writer, Michael Henderson, worked himself into a lather over the accent of the then England cricket captain, Nasser Hussein. 'Somebody who went to a good university has no excuse for speaking in that ghastly estuary sludge,' he grumbled—and you just knew that, for him at least, the *ah* of *ghahstly* would go on for ever. Poor old Hussein had presumably attracted his attention with the hang-overs in his accent from his childhood in Ilford, Essex: on his retirement as England captain, he told journalists he had found that age was *catchin' up on me a litt-uw bi'*, and in his Press conference, the *a* sounds in words like *major* and *days* came out as a London *eye*. Speaking of his retirement, he said: *i' has been a mijor thing f' me*. Henderson presumably thought that Durham University should have straightened up his vowels and had them standing on parade ready for inspection—and if a 'good university' was not sufficient to turn Hussein into a gentleman, then perhaps he should have followed the example of his predecessor of the 1950s, Len Hutton. He was said to have taken elocution lessons to take the edges off his broad Yorkshire accent when he became England captain. But those days are gone.

It's sad to think what a slavish adherence to Received Pronunciation might have done to the commentaries of John Arlott, whose soft, luxuriant Hampshire accent caressed his words with the subtlety of one of Hussein's own perfectly-timed off-drives. Arlott himself told the story of how, in 1948, the BBC's Head of Outside Broadcasting told him: 'You have an interesting mind, but a vulgar voice.'[11] Would Geoffrey Boycott have been a better batsman if he had spoken like a BBC announcer? Nasser Hussein, if he had bothered to reply to Henderson's attack, would no doubt have said that he wanted to be a cricketer, not an elocutionist or a butler. He might have asked why his Essex accent was less desirable than Arlott's Hampshire. Or he might simply have observed, as many people whose speech is criticized might do, that Henderson was simply being bloody rude and offensive. People often forget about good manners when they concentrate on good diction.

So we are coming towards an understanding of what Shaw meant—why it is that every time someone opens his mouth, someone else starts to despise him. The way we speak reveals who we are, but it also reveals, much more tellingly, who we want to be. What Nasser Hussein's voice said was that he wasn't interested in becoming what Michael Henderson thought he ought to be. And poor old Sir Thomas Elyot, worrying nearly 500 years ago about the dangers to his children's accents from 'foolish women', actually had it exactly wrong. At least according to modern academic linguists, women are *more* likely than men to lose their regional accents. There are fairly obvious reasons why they might choose to do so: repeated surveys suggest that women who speak RP are thought to be more competent, more independent, more successful and of course, more likely to get a job from a modern Sir Thomas. Similar considerations, of course, might apply to men—but then, regional or non-standard accents are also seen as bringing with them elements of roughness, toughness and machismo. The rise of 'ladette culture'—girls who look like Alice in Wonderland but talk like Wayne Rooney and drink like Paul Gascoigne—might make the balance change as they become keener to display their own roughness and toughness with the way they speak. Boys will be boys, and so, increasingly, will girls. People don't always want to be what you might expect.

At the other end of the social scale, people avoid RP for different reasons. Linguists have searched for different words to describe the exaggerated version that is spoken among the upper classes: maybe the best is Refined Received Pronunciation, or RRP. There is no pretence that RRP is particularly pure or accurate: it exists simply to set its users apart. Just like gum-chewing youngsters who don't want to sound like their parents, so speakers of RRP don't want to sound like the rest of the world. Occasionally this is stated openly— Lord Brocket was thoroughly delighted on television with his own 'toff's accent'—but more often, it's simply taken for granted.

It may be a clichéd description of the true gentleman, but the maverick former Conservative minister and diarist Alan Clark never insulted anyone without meaning to— and he never hid his desire to accentuate the difference between himself and everybody else either. In an interview shortly before his death in 1999, he spoke his own exaggerated RRP English, just as he always did. In his throaty, upper-class drawl, he talked about how *lahvleh* his young wife had looked on her wedding day—or, as he put it, the day he was *ma'ied*. He choked so hard on his *r*'s that it was hard to tell whether he thought that politics was resistible or irresistible—*i'isistible*, as he put it, gurgling over the beginning of the word from the intimate depths of his throat. Most people, in an unconscious effort to please the person they are speaking to, will adapt their accent slightly to suit the circumstances—but not Clark. Even in the relaxed atmosphere of the interview, his accent was, so to speak, wearing a collar and tie, his *a*'s so rounded and full that they could barely get out of his mouth: 'Nice guys always finish lahss' don't they?' he asked. He recalled later that he had once told the prime minister, Margaret Thatcher, how he had studied her figure admiringly as she leaned forward over the Despatch Box, and noticed that she had *ve'y pretty ee-ankles*. He added, just as convinced but slightly less convincingly, 'She rather enjoyed thee-at.'

Well, perhaps—but if people laughed at the way Clark spoke, he didn't care. And he was not alone in his embracing of RRP: Lord Charles Powell, former private secretary to Lady Thatcher in 10 Downing Street, has, unlike his two brothers, adopted the idiosyncratic pronunciation 'Pole' for his surname, and he still speaks RRP with an aristocratic drawl. He is the son of an Air Vice-Marshal in the Royal Air Force, and something of a Tory grandee in his own right—and he sounds it. In a recent radio interview, for instance, he talked about his time as private secretary to Lady *Thetchah*, commented on the presidency in the US of Jimmy *Cartah*, and referred to the *overlepping* concerns of his foreign affairs and defence briefs in Number 10.

It's not what you say, in fact, it's the way that you say it—and there have always been people prepared to say exactly how you *should* say it. Early in the twentieth century, King William IV's grand-daughter, the Countess of Munster—than whom there were few people more elevated, even in that age of aristocratic grandeur—laid down the pronunciation of the word *girl* as one important test of true social quality. 'The higher classes pronounce it as if it were spelt *gairl*, whereas the vulgar pronounce it as if it were spelt *gurl*,' she wrote.[12] Presumably no one dared to ask why. The distinction still just about survives today, among the self-consciously upper-class mothers of 'young gels', although it has been cruelly lampooned for decades. *Gurl* as a pronunciation of *ir* does at least compare with *bird*, *irk*, *whirl* or *twirl*, but the vowel in *gairl* seems to be oddly Scottish or Irish, or even Scouse. But of course, the point is that it is none of those things: it is a pronunciation that is affected simply because it is different, because it sets 'the higher classes' apart from the rest.

The same is true of many of the sounds of RRP. Some of them, like the exaggeratedly opened *u* sound that makes *fun* sound almost like *fan*, are simply standard pronunciations taken to an extreme, while others seem to be designed to show how people of power and influence can ignore the rules which are applied slightly lower down the social scale. In ordinary RP, for instance, pronouncing a final *-ing* as *-in'* would be seen as a definite black mark, one of the clear signs of non-U-ness, along with dropped *h*'s and rounded *u*'s—but the aristocracy really did once talk about *huntin'*, *shootin'* and *fishin'*. Even the *h*'s weren't safe: the late Queen Mother, launching one of her many ships, would habitually say 'May God bless 'er and all who sail in 'er,' while Winston Churchill would use the phrase *at 'ome* where a lesser man might have said *at home*. The actor John Gielgud, who usually managed to sound infinitely more royal than the royals, would pronounce words like *humour* and *human* with a grand initial *yu*.

Other RRP habits are truly distinctive pronunciations. Vowels are mysteriously stretched to breaking point, so *that man* becomes *thee-at mee-an*, like Mrs Thatcher's *ee-ankles*. The sound which phonologists cheerfully name the 'happy vowel'—the *i* at the end of words like *silly*, *funny* or *happy*— may be opened to an *-eh*, while the *o* in *cloth* or *toss* stretches out into *or*. Princess Anne, telling photographers to 'Naff off,' was not simply introducing a grateful nation to a new and useful word (it's alleged to come from Polari, a secret gay slang spoken by homosexuals during the mid-twentieth century, and to be an acronym meaning someone who was not sympathetic, and therefore Not Available For—well, you get the point) but also giving them an object lesson in two of the key vowels of RRP. *Nee-aff orff*. Among the truly *refaned*, *wine* can often sound like *wane*: perhaps it is seen as a mark of breeding to avoid anything so common as an *eye* vowel like the ones Cockneys use to describe *the rine in Spine*.

But even the members of the Royal Family have modified their RRP: the Queen's English is now much more like that of the majority of her subjects than it was in the days when she said *hice* for *house* and referred to her daughter *Enn*. What used to be common habits, such as the *-ah* of *Indiah* or *waitah*, are now more often heard in comedy shows and parodies than in real life—although the judge's *Har'f'dshee-ah* endured as a happy exception. Refined Received Pronunciation still survives—or rather, *survayves*—but it is on the retreat.

One reason for its decline is that those who do speak it tend to become figures of fun. Jacob Rees-Mogg, the Old-Etonian son of the former *Times* editor Lord Rees-Mogg, has an RP accent which is so Refined that it is almost off the scale—and which was generally agreed to have been a disadvantage in his search for a seat as a Conservative MP. He has complained wistfully that 'It is rather pathetic to fuss about accents too much.' That's probably true, although a cynic might observe that anyone who didn't want to be lampooned might have been well advised not to have campaigned in a safe Labour seat in a Rolls-Royce, and with his old nanny for company. If he wanted to end prejudice based on the way people speak, Rees-Mogg might also have done well to swallow his own observation that 'John Prescott's accent marks him out as an oaf.'[13]

39

So times have changed. Bullies have always enjoyed using language to beat their victims over the head—but nowadays, it isn't only the toffs who beat up the oiks. One of New Labour's bright-as-a-button female back-benchers, Julie Morgan, was challenged on Radio 4's *Today* programme over the government's intention to impose a smoking ban in pubs throughout England by the artist David Hockney, whose Bradford accent is at least as broad as it is long. Ms Morgan certainly doesn't speak Rees-Moggian, but she boasts impeccable New Labour credentials—postgraduate degree in social administration, former social worker, and local Labour councillor—and she was slowly and carefully explaining what the government was planning to do, with Hockney's booming Yorkshire interruptions practically drowning her out. 'Yer too bosseh, choom! Yer dreareh! Yer bosseh!' Hockney repeated, leaving her in confusion. It wasn't just his standing as an internationally famous artist that enabled him to bully the unfortunate politician so shamelessly; it wasn't even just his rudeness in shouting her down, or the brutal loudness of his voice. It was, as much as anything, the heavy northern accent, with its voice-of-the-people overtones, that left Ms Morgan speechless.

Hockney's successful bullying suggests one reason why not everyone speaks RP. After all, if so many people see the social and professional advantages of 'speaking proper'—if they want them for their children—why don't they all seize them for themselves? A few unrounded *u*'s, rounded *a*'s and carefully-preserved aspirates might seem a small price to pay. But in fact, the advantages are not all one way. For a start, RP, like other accents of English, has gathered its own stereotypes along the way. If surveys suggest that speakers of regional accents are less intelligent and successful than speakers of RP, they also suggest that they are seen as more open and friendly. Those tasty little round cakes that you sometimes get with strawberry jam and clotted cream are relevant here—a recent survey suggested that they can be pronounced either *sc-o-nn* with a short *o*, rhyming with *gone*, or *sc-oh-n*, with a long one, rhyming with *cone*. The short *o* is probably more common in Scotland and the north of England, and the long one in the south, but the two pronunciations are scattered across the country. And the interesting thing is that most people think that the one they *don't* use is the 'posh' one.

Far from being an accentless, 'correct' form of English, RP is seen from outside as an accent which has overtones of arrogance, lack of sympathy, and even cruelty. Hollywood producers whose careers would be in tatters if they allowed a Native American in their

41

movies to hold up one hand and say, 'How! Me Big Chief Sitting Bull!' habitually cast their creepiest villains as Englishmen speaking in cut-glass tones which are every bit as anachronistic. If speakers of RRP are cast as clowns, then speakers of RP are villains. One day, perhaps an upper-crust Englishman will sue a Hollywood film company just to make the point.

But the more important reason why not everyone will speak RP is slightly more complex. Most people have no trouble in holding two ideas in their heads at the same time, and while they see the advantages of RP both for themselves and their children, they also want to retain a sense of themselves. As we'll see in the next few chapters, there are still regional accents all over Britain. Some people want to hide where they came from as avidly as they hide their tax returns, but generally, the truth seems to be that if the way we speak reveals who we want to be, then most of us don't want to be someone entirely different from the person we were born. Only a tiny percentage of people speak RP—but many more speak some form of modified RP which reflects their native accent. They accept some aspects of it, but prefer to retain something of their past as well, levelling out the way they talk, like slapping plaster on a rough stone wall to leave just a few slight bumps and undulations behind. Norman Rees, the respected ITN news correspondent, worked hard as a young man to smooth the corners of the broad Cardiff accent he had as a child—but still sounds clearly and contentedly Welsh. 'I was amazed when I first heard myself on a tape recorder. I just wasn't comfortable with my voice—there was this harsh *air* sound in words like *Cardiff* that I just didn't know I had. I had an elocution teacher after I started in television who helped me to concentrate on that one vowel, and then I'd practise it on my own, from morning to night,' he says. 'What I ended up with was the Welsh accent I'd always thought I had, before I ever heard myself on tape.' Nasser Hussein's voice may not please old buffers writing in the *Daily Telegraph*, but he, too, speaks a perfectly comprehensible and 'correct' English with, in his case, an overlay of the Essex town in which he grew up.

Joan Bakewell, who wrote in her autobiography[14] about her embarrassment over her Lancashire accent as a young student in the 1950s Cambridge of 'braying, honking tones that indicated class and money', also struggled to change the way she spoke. 'After a while, nature reasserts itself, and your natural accent begins to come back, so that you find a sort of halfway house where you feel comfortable,' she says now. Today, she revels in the mixture of accents about her home in Central London. 'There are so many people from foreign countries, speaking with Polish accents, German, French. And then there are the lovely lilting Asian voices, and the Caribbean inflections. The variety in speech is enormous these days, and it's growing,' she says.

And a good thing too. A world of impeccably 'correct' English, without regional accents or changing pronunciations would be like living on a never-ending diet of candy-floss, or spending your life in a lift listening to the muzak.

*　　*　　*

If you can't pronounce the names of people like Cholmondley or Featherstonehaugh properly (*Chumley* and *Fanshaw*, if you should ever want to call) then you probably aren't the sort of person they want visiting them anyway. But it is not just in sorting out the social wheat from the chaff that accents and pronunciation are used as a crude rule of thumb. Whether it is music, art, food, drink or even sport, there is no faster way to lose credibility than to pronounce the words wrongly. Sailors have their own private transatlantic squabble over their mutually incomprehensible pronunciations of *buoy*, with the Americans laughing at the English for pronouncing the word *boy*, while the English raise their eyebrows at the *boo-ey* of the Americans. If either of them bothered to read the four letters, they would presumably say something like *bwoy*—but logic and reason have little to do with pronunciation. In that example, each side can generally accept the bizarre behaviour of the other with no more than a good-natured shrug of the shoulders— but other pronunciations could have you practically thrown out of the yacht club. Woe to the would-be sailor who talks about a *main sail* rather than a *mains'l*, or a *hal-yard* instead of a *haly'd*, or who imagines that a *Genoa* sail will be pronounced in the same way as the city of the same name. (It's a *GEN-oa*, rather than a *GenOH-a*, if anyone with half a brain cares. There may be those who argue about the English pronunciation of the Italian city, but it was settled for all time by the music hall joke. 'I met my wife in Italy—Genoa?—Well, I do now.') *Rowlocks*, of course, should always be pronounced as if they were spelled with a double-*ll* rather than a *w*. (Decency forbids me to suggest the only rhyme I can think of.)

It's not as deadly as the *bandura-banadura* or *Aitch Samuel-Haitch Samuel* games of the Lebanese and Irish gunmen, but it has its roots in the same malicious desire to establish who is with us and who is not—who is one of the *cognoscenti* (always pronounced, of course, with a properly Italian *conyo-*). H. E. Bateman never drew a cartoon of the young man at a Royal Philharmonic concert who pronounced Haydn, Beethoven, Dvorak or Sibelius as their names are spelled, but he should have done. Is there an educated person alive who has never read the famous Russian novel *Worn Piece*? Alan Bennett allowed himself a superior little snigger when a radio announcer referred to the opera *La Fille Mal Gardée* as *The Female Gardee*.[15] Elsewhere, Luis Buñuel's classic film *L'Age D'Or* becomes, more prosaically, *Large Door*. In the art gallery, there is another transatlantic difference of opinion, with Englishmen sniggering at the way Americans talk of *Van Goh*, when of course they mean *Van Goff*. They are both wrong, of course— Van Gogh would have pronounced his name, as his descendants still do, with a guttural sound like the Scottish *loch*. Small wonder that he should have declared that he didn't want to hear his name butchered by art dealers, and simply signed his work *Vincent*.

Go out to eat and you can choke on the words before you even get to your *hors d'oeuvres*. In France, *clairet* was once used to distinguish light-coloured (*clair*) wine from the deep red of—er—claret, but the English borrowed the word some time in the fifteenth century. It was long enough ago for them not only to change the meaning, but also to add a final *t* to the pronunciation just to show their disdain for the airy-fairy French original. I have spoken to an assistant at Fortnum & Mason who swears that he has been faced by an anxious-looking American customer, misled by the seductive *-et*, who demanded to know his opinion of the *clarray*. But just try pronouncing the final *t* of *merlot* or *pinot* in an expensive restaurant and watch the wine waiter's sneer. And then, once you have decided that despite the pronunciation of *claret*, you should make the final *t*'s silent like the French do, you come to the fish course. If you ask for *turbot* as if it were the option on a Saab, you will probably be moved to a table where none of the other diners can hear you, if you are allowed to stay at all.

Sometimes, of course, it's possible to get across the message that you don't *want* to be part of a particular group. The BBC *Newsnight* presenter who was reviewing the papers on the night when the well-known French Manchester United footballer Eric Cantona was in the news, read the headline *Oo-ah CanTONa* with precisely the same bemused but superior curl of the lip that the famous judge must have had when he asked, 'Exactly what *is* an iPod?' The slightest sensitivity to the metrical subtleties of football chants should have told the presenter that only *Can-ton-AH* could come after *oo-ah*—but the point he was making was that he was much more at home in the political section than he would ever be in the sports pages.

Perhaps the same presenter would refer to José Mourinho, the manager of Chelsea, as if he pronounced his name in the same way as José Carreras, the famous tenor. The trouble is, as the most ignorant Chelsea fan could tell him, Maurinho is Portuguese, and so pronounces the *J*, while Carreras is Spanish, and so calls himself *Hosay*. How are you supposed to be aware of any of these things? You're not, unless you're in the know. That's the point of all of it, RP, French menus, and struggling, strangled vowels alike—they show that you are one of us.

CHAPTER TWO

A Patchwork of Voices
Regional accents in England—where they come from and what they mean

One of the quickest ways of announcing which group you belong to and which you don't is to speak with a regional accent. It tells whereabouts in the country you come from, of course, but, as Hilda Reid, Lady Chatterley's dense sister in *Lady Chatterley's Lover*, found out, it tells more than that as well.

'"Why do you speak Yorkshire?" she said softly.

'"That! That's non Yorkshire, that's Derby." He looked back at her with that faint, distant grin.

'"Derby, then! Why do you speak Derby? You spoke natural English at first."

'"Did Ah though? An 'canna Ah change if Ah'm a mind to 't? Nay, nay, let me talk Derby if it suits me. If yo'n nowt against it."'

There are no straight lines and no firm boundaries in language, and there are many different variations of northern accents: Yorkshire speech fades into Derbyshire, and to that extent, Hilda's mistake is understandable. But the real boundary she is referring to, the one that is marked out by language in *Lady*

49

Chatterley's Lover, is not geographical but social. Earlier in the book, Oliver Mellors, the gamekeeper, explains to Connie that he can slip from one accent into another, but that he had made a positive choice to reject what Hilda called 'natural English' and the middle-class life that went with it. 'I stopped talking "fine", as they call it, talking proper English, and went back to talking broad,' he says.

Though Lawrence was writing nearly eighty years ago, there is still a clear class element in the differences between RP and the various accents of the regions. Generally, the higher up the social scale you go in England, the less marked are the regional accents you are likely to find.

English, like every other language, has always been blown by winds from every direction. The way we speak has been affected by other languages, by the movement of people, by fashion, by new discoveries, by social and economic pressures—but on 14 November 1922, there was a new influence which seemed likely to outweigh everything that had gone before it.

The crackly sound of the BBC's Station 2LO, broadcasting from the seventh floor of Marconi House in London's Strand for one hour a day, was the first time anyone had spoken to the whole nation. From those uncertain beginnings would grow a service which would eventually speak not just to every social class and to all the different regions of the country, with all their varying local accents, but to every part of the world. For centuries, the printed word had set uniform standards of writing and spelling across the country: now it looked as though the same thing might happen to the spoken word.

From the earliest days, the solemn panjandrums who managed what was then the British Broadcasting Company were deeply conscious of what the future Lord Reith termed 'the problems of spoken English'. He said: 'One hears the most appalling travesties of vowel production. This is a matter in which broadcasting may be of immense assistance,'[16] and even though he promised rather unconvincingly that there was no intention to establish a uniform spoken language, the dinner-jacketed announcers behind the BBC microphones set about defining a standard of correctness for pronunciation that would eventually find its way into every home in the land. 'The policy might be described as that of seeking a common denominator of educated speech,' Lord Reith declared.[17]

People had been pontificating for centuries about how words should be pronounced and spelled, about where stresses should be placed and how vowels should be sounded, but they had never enjoyed such a powerful weapon. Where they had been limited to descriptions of how they believed the language should be spoken—which, of course, were only seen by those who read their books anyway—the BBC would demonstrate its 'common denominator of educated speech' every day, as a model of 'correct' speech.

Twenty years after Lord Reith's linguistic manifesto, many people believed that one of the effects of the BBC's power would be the death of regional and local accents. The broadcaster Wilfred Pickles, born in Halifax and with a Yorkshire accent you could have boiled tripe in, found the prospect horrifying: 'How terrible it is to think that we may some day lose that lovely soft Devonshire accent or the bluff and very wonderful Scots brogue or the amusing flatness and forthrightness of the North-countryman's speech, or the music of the Welsh voice,' he said. 'May it be forbidden that we should ever speak like BBC announcers, for our rich contrast of voices is a vocal tapestry of great beauty and incalculable value, handed down to us by our forefathers.'[18]

He was carefully being nice about everyone, but he was also, of course, setting up stereotypes of his own: that 'lovely soft Devonshire accent' sounds a little less soft when the speaker is in a towering rage, and most North-countrymen would be more than flat and forthright if they were told patronizingly how amusing they were. Tacking character traits on to accents is a dangerous game. But at least Wilfred Pickles was speaking from some experience—called on to read the news during the Second World War, because security chiefs in the government believed that the Germans might find it more difficult to mimic his broad northern accent, he faced a barrage of criticism from listeners and mockery in the newspapers. 'Lahst a thing of the pahst' was one headline, and a cartoon showed him sitting in front of his microphone with his cloth cap and woollen muffler and saying, 'Here is the news, and ee bah gum, this is Wilfred Pickles reading it.' Some listeners claimed that they couldn't believe the news when it was read in such a broad accent.

But he needn't have worried about the future of the language. There is an unalterable natural law that things never turn out as you expect, and the disaster he was warning of didn't happen—or at least, not in the way that he feared. Yes, the BBC established its own worldwide standard of speech and pronunciation—BBC English, its own version of Received Pronunciation—but at the same time, the regional accents which Wilfred Pickles spoke up for so passionately had their own effect upon the broadcasters.

The corpse of BBC English took a little time to lie down and be still, but the opening of the airwaves to independent television companies in the mid-1950s was an early nail in its coffin. The first newsreader for the new

Independent Television News, Christopher Chataway, seemed to be cast in the traditional BBC mould—Sherborne School, Magdalen College, Oxford, and a career ahead of him as a Conservative minister, with an upper-crust accent to match—but the network of reporters around him reflected a new age. Local TV companies had been appointing local staff, and when the new network service needed reporters, they turned to them. Instead of the clipped tones of a self-conscious elite, the relaxed sounds of northern, Scottish, western and Welsh accents could be heard every day on the growing numbers of television sets—at least when they were tuned to the independent stations. Whatever Lord Reith may have dreamed of, 'educated speech' didn't seem to be restricted to Received Pronunciation—and when, in 1977, the Annan Report on the future of broadcasting rather defensively commented, 'We welcome regional accents,' it marked the replacement of the old model of BBC English by the new English of ITV.

In most of today's BBC, the Reithian search for a 'common denominator' has been abandoned—up to a point. Anyone who doubts the commitment to the Annan Report's welcome for regional accents need only remember John Cole, the BBC's former political editor, who was mercilessly lampooned in *Private Eye* because of the way he spoke, but who is generally accepted to be one of the most respected and well-connected correspondents the Corporation ever had. He spoke with the same broad Belfast accent he had all his life—so that, according to one senior producer, there was one occasion where, playing back a tape of his own voice, he was unable to make out his own words. 'The scree-ut Prime Munister,' the tape said, quite clearly. Cole and the producer listened again: there was no doubt. 'The scree-ut Prime Munister.' It was only after some time that the two men finally cracked the code, and understood the message: Cole had been talking about 'This great Prime Minister.'

Viewers seemed to like Cole's accent: there was certainly no suggestion from the BBC's log that anyone felt, as they had claimed to feel in the 1940s about Wilfred Pickles's northern voice, that they couldn't trust what he said. But John Cole was the exception rather than the rule. Although a viewer can now hear a variety of regional accents on news programmes, they are generally only slightly different from the BBC norm. A Welsh lilt or a flat northern *a* here and a West Country *r* there hardly add up to a determined commitment to embrace the whole range of British speech—and in the national newsroom, among off-screen journalists as much as on-screen presenters and correspondents, you will go a long way before you hear a strong regional accent. To that extent at least, Lord

Reith lives on.

* * *

Asking why so many regional accents of English grew up is starting from the wrong place. The question suggests that there is some standard norm from which these different accents have somehow diverged—and if this book has one single message, it is that, while there may be accents that have more or less social prestige, there is no norm. And, as we'll see, whatever divergences there may have been are not always in the direction you might expect.

You can often see a line of ancestry from the regional speech of today back to the particular form of English that was spoken centuries ago. North of a line from the Lune to the Humber, for instance, are the distinctive north-east accents of Geordie, Mackem and Pitmatic, the accents spoken around Newcastle, Sunderland and Northumberland. One suggestion is that the name 'Geordie' was a mocking reference to the way the people of Newcastle supported King George II during Bonnie Prince Charlie's rebellion of 1745. Mackem is a modern name, which isn't seen in print before the 1990s, and Pitmatic was originally the language of the pits of the Durham and Northumberland coalfields. Anyone from outside the region might find it

56

hard to tell them apart, and it's probably safest not to try—but they share a history that goes right back to the Old English of the Northumbrian kingdom, and the Germanic languages of the Angles and Vikings. It's often suggested, though with no clear evidence, that visitors from Norway and Sweden find it easier to understand these dialects, with their distinctive vowel sounds, than the more conventional speech of the south-east.

Certainly, the Norman invasion of 1066 had less effect here than it did further south, and it is easy to see the way that Scottish influence has turned *ow* sounds into *oo*, so that *town* is pronounced *toon*, or *brown* becomes *broon*. Probably the most easily recognizable feature is the way double vowels are split: *when the boat comes in* becomes *when the boh-ut comes in*; your ear is your *ea-uh*. Flat *a*'s generally become short *e*'s, so that *that* is pronounced *thet*, or *have* is pronounced *hev*, although *man* is generally pronounced somewhere between *man* and *mon*. There are also aspects of the accent that are unique to the area—while it is common for regional accents to say *-in'* instead of *-ing* at the end of a word, for instance, the north-east is the only place where that changes to *-un*. The Newcastle United footballer Alan Shearer told interviewers that when he had to go off in what turned out to be his last Premiership match, he was 'hopun' and 'prayun'' that his injury wouldn't be serious.

Hopun', mind, not *'opun'*—the north-east is also one of very few parts of the country where dropping initial *h*'s is not a feature of casual speech. *House* is pronounced *hoos*, but never *'oos*. Anyone who can't imagine a toned-down north-eastern accent needs only to think of Ant and Dec or the *Big Brother* voice-over.

There is an important distinction to be made between dialects and accents. Apart from the distinctive pronunciation they left behind, the Angles, Vikings, Scots and Northumbrians also left individual words which survive in the north-east but aren't used elsewhere in England, so that children are *bairns*, dirty is *hacky*, and *howay—howay the lads!*—means *come on!* There are also particular survivals of grammar and syntax which would be unfamiliar elsewhere, so that *us* might be used instead of *me*, and there are distinctive past tenses of many verbs, so that *took* might be used instead of *taken, tellt* instead of *told*, or *putten* instead of *put*. There is a famous story of a schoolteacher who pointed to a word in her pupil's book and asked what the mistake was. The boy thought for a moment, then slapped his forehead in exasperation and said, 'Oh, miss, I've been and putten *putten* where I should have putten *put*.' Dialects have their own vocabularies and grammatical structures—different past tenses and the use of a direct instead of an indirect object, for instance, so they say *I give it 'im*, rather than *I gave it to him*—while accent is concerned only with the sound of the words and the rhythm and intonation of the sentence. In the last example, using *give* for *gave* and missing out *to* are differences of dialect, but saying *'im* instead of *him* is a difference of accent.

Accents, like dialects, for that matter, tend to blend into each other from one region to another. Giving them different names suggests that there might be some sort of border, almost like Hadrian's Wall, with one vowel sound on one side and another on the other. There are clear Scottish elements in the accents of the north-east of England that are not found anywhere further south—but there are also characteristics that are easily recognizable throughout the rest of the northern region.

The rounded northern *u*, for example, which has the same vowel sound in *cup* as it has in *put*, is found all over the north, and the splitting of double vowels that is a feature in the north-east is also found much further south. In the south-east of England, *meet* and *meat* would sound exactly the same, but in different parts of the northern region, *meat* might be pronounced *mee-ut*, or *mayt*. And then, of course, there is the flat northern *a*— the one which goes with flat caps, mufflers, and a rounded *u* to create the southerners' idea of life in the north of England. That, too, can be found in the north-east, hiding away among the Scottish vowel sounds.

It is the flat *a* and the rounded *u* which for many people define a northern accent, although both pronunciations are actually used far more widely than just in the north of England, and of course, there are many other 'northern' features which vary across the region. There is a story about a librarian in Barrow-in-Furness, Cumbria, for instance, who was puzzled by a man who came in and asked in a broad northern accent, 'Have you a book about the shores?' She took him over to the section on physical geography, where he looked around half-heartedly and bemusedly for a moment or two, before turning to her and saying, 'No, I meant the *shores*—the shores like *Kiss Me Kate* or *Me and My Girl . . .*'

Another woman couldn't understand what her friend—from the other side of the Pennines this time—had been doing in an Indian restaurant when she told her that she had been so drunk she was 'practically in a korma'. Across Cumbria, Lancashire, and much of Yorkshire, the *oh*-sound is widened almost to *or*, so that shows become shores and comas become kormas. In other parts of South and West Yorkshire, the same *oh* vowel might come out as *oi*, producing the famous Yorkshire song:

We're reight dahn i't'coil 'oil wheer t'muck

60

slarts on't winders.
We've used all o't'coil an' we're reight dahn
t't cinders.
When t'bum bailiff comes 'e'll nivver find
us,
'Cos we're reight dahn i't'coil 'oil wheer
t'muck slarts on't winders.

The *er* sound replacing a final *oh* is common too, which can lead to complications for people trying to change the way they speak— like the small boy I remember when I was a child, talking about looking in the 'mirroh'. He'd been told off so often for talking about 'pillers' rather than 'pillows', and about 'winders' rather than 'windows', that he wasn't going to make the same mistake with the mirror. It's called hyper-correction—being so anxious not to make a mistake that you go too far in the other direction. Sir John Gielgud, who talked so precisely about *actORS*, would not have understood the problem, but Alan Bennett, the Leeds-born playwright, would. He wrote about the difficulties he experienced: 'I tried to lose my northern accent at one period, then reacquired it, and now don't know where I am, sometimes saying my *a*'s long, sometimes short, and *u*'s a continuing threat, words like *butcher* and names like *Cutbush* always lying in ambush. Anyone who ventures south of the Trent is likely to contract an incurable disease of the vowels . . .'[19]

Perhaps he shouldn't have bothered: many phonologists[20] estimate that something like half the population of England have some elements of what would be considered northern speech in their accent.

Accents in England probably split most clearly between north and south—but then, exactly where do people mean by 'north'? The line—and, as we noted above, it is a very blurred and fuzzy line—separating those who pronounce their *u*'s with a northern *oo* from those in the south who see a distinction between the vowels in *put* and *cup* runs roughly from the Severn estuary in the west to the Wash in the east. A similar line drawn to mark the extent of the flat *a* would run more or less in the same direction, but slightly further north.

Generalizations are dangerous, of course, and there are significant differences between the different accents to be found within that northern area, such as Scouse, Brummie and Yorkshire. The towns of Barnsley and Sheffield in South Yorkshire are only fifteen miles apart, but no one who lives in either town would mistake one accent for the other. Barnsley people talk about Sheffield *dee-dahs* because of the Sheffield accent which talks, according to one local newspaper editor, of 'dis, dat, and sometimes de udder'. Barnsley vowels tend to be much longer—*ree-ut, then* (*right then*) rather than *rit, den* in Sheffield;

schoolchildren go to *scoo-il* in Barnsley, and to *scoyl* in Sheffield; and while Barnsley people will tell you they live in *Bay-ernsleh*, a Sheffield speaker would call it *Bornsleh*. Brian Sheridan, a local expert who has lived all his life in South Yorkshire, claims to be able to distinguish people from Chesterfield, Barnsley, Doncaster and Sheffield—four towns within twenty miles of each other—with ease. But to people from outside the region, any accent with a flat *a* and a rounded *u* sounds simply 'northern'. A condescending London journalist observed about Pauline Prescott, the wife of the deputy prime minister, with staggering rudeness, that she was really quite sophisticated, and didn't have a trace of a Yorkshire accent—which, bearing in mind that she comes from Chester, far away on the other side of the Pennines, should hardly have been a surprise. But then, you wouldn't expect a journalist who lives his entire life south of Watford and sees the M25 as the frontier of civilization to realize that there is a difference.

There are, too, plenty of people throughout the region who don't pronounce their vowels in a northern way at all, and many others who would habitually use a flat *a*, but would think it decidedly infra dig to round their *u*'s in words like *brother*, *butter* or *something*. Even so, and accepting the local differences between one town and another across the whole region, it's clear that, at least as far as language is concerned, the north of England runs deep into the Midlands.

But however far south it stretches, what happened to make the north different? Are these distinctive northern vowels a deviation from some more 'correct' form of English that still survives in the south? Certainly in the case of the rounded *u*, what happened seems to have been quite complicated—but it was in the south-east, not the north, that the change came. In Middle English—that is, around the fourteenth and fifteenth centuries—everyone spoke with a northern *u*. During the following 200 years or so, this seems to have split into two separate sounds in the south of England, opening into a modern *uh* in most cases, but retaining its original rounded *oo* after consonants such as *p* or *f*, which are pronounced with the lips. That explains why a southern pronunciation would have different vowel sounds in *dull* and *full*, in *cut* and in *put*, or in *rush* and *push*.

Or at least, that's the simple explanation—there are a lot of exceptions. *M* and *n*, for instance, seem to cancel out the effect of an initial *p* or *f*, so that, in the south at least, *pun* and *fun* have a different vowel sound from *pull* and *full*. A *b* at the start of a word is pronounced with the lips, so we have *bull* where the *u* is rounded—but southerners also have *butter* and *but*, where it isn't. In some parts of the north, a *k* at the end of the word will lengthen the *u*, so that *book* or *cook* have almost the same vowel as a word like *coop*. People follow whatever rules they grew up with, but they would usually be hard-pressed to explain what they are.

The new open *u* spread across the country during the early eighteenth century as new fashions do, moving from city to city, and then gradually becoming accepted in the rural areas between. According to one theory, though, Birmingham was the last major conurbation on the way north, so it was impossible for the open *u* to spread further. To the north, the traditional rounded *u* survived—and still does.

Much the same was happening, around the same time, to the *a* sound. As late as the eighteenth century, words such as *pass*, *bath* and *castle* were all generally pronounced with a short, 'northern' vowel—the same vowel that travelled to North America with the Pilgrim Fathers a hundred years or so before, and so survives in most of the United States. Towards the end of the century, speakers in London started to lengthen the vowel, so the words became *pahth*, *bahth* and *cahstle*. The rounded *a* spread out from London, just as its cousin, the unrounded *u*, had done, picked up in town after town. At least until the late nineteenth century, it was bitterly criticized as a vulgar, Cockney affectation—but despite that, rural areas between the towns gradually picked up the new fad, just as they had with the unrounded *u*, until within a hundred years or so, the fashion had swept across the country.

Or rather, across about half the country. Birmingham, once again, was an impassable barrier, and the flat *a* survived through the midlands and the north. In the west, the distinction becomes meaningless, as all the *a* sounds come in a wide western *ar*, so there is hardly any distinction between the vowel in *pat*, which southerners and northerners alike would pronounce with a flat *a*, and *path*, where the split would be obvious. Anyone who has stood in the crowd to watch Gloucester play rugby, and has heard the long, beery shouts of 'Glaaaarssss!' will recognize at once that it is not only the *a* vowels that get the full *ar* treatment in the west country.

The one thing that isn't to be found in the whole situation is logic. A native of Birmingham, who might instinctively pronounce *finger* to rhyme with *linger*, might point to the words *singer* and *single*, or, come to that, to *linger* and *lingerie*, and ask what rule determines why some sound the *g* and others don't. There isn't a reason. That obstinate *g* is a habit, like the flat *a* of northern England, that is very resistant to change, so that people brought up in the Midlands who have lost most of the traces of their original accents will often still have a slight guttural stop in the middle of *singer*. Again, it's not a new habit that has grown up, but the survival of a way of speaking that used to be common across the country: phonologists believe that the final *g* in *-ing* would have been pronounced in most educated accents of English up to the seventeenth century. Even now, many people all over the country will sometimes sound it and sometimes not in the middle of *England* and *language*.

A northerner might similarly ask someone from the south-east how anyone is supposed to know that you say *clahss* and *clahssroom* with rounded *a*'s, but then go on to say *classify* with a flat one. And how would they explain *pahss* and *pahssport* but *passage*? Or *cushion*, where the *u* is rounded, but *percussion*, where it's not? But there is no room for complacency further north—how would northerners explain the fact that, unlike Americans, many of them say *cahn't* with a rounded *a*, rather than *cann't* with a flat one, and *banahna* rather than *bananna*? After all, everybody says *bandanna* rather than *bandahna*. Many northerners, too, would say *plaster* and *disaster*, with flat *a*'s, but would happily round the same vowel in *mahster*. Others, of course, would happily stick with *master*, with a flat *a*. And in strong regional dialect, still others might lengthen the vowel to *maister*. 'Maister, maister, he's staling t'lanthern!' shouts Heathcliff's servant Joseph, in the first few pages of *Wuthering Heights*.

It doesn't necessarily take hundreds of years to form a distinctive regional accent. The name for the distinctive Liverpool accent, Scouse, comes originally from Labskause, a Danish word for a sort of Irish stew from Finland, and that just about sums up its cosmopolitan origins. There is no record of the word being used to describe the accent rather than the stew before the 1960s, and Scouse itself, probably one of the most recognizable English accents, has a history that goes back no further than a century and a half, to the large-scale Irish immigration into Liverpool caused by the Irish Potato Famine of the mid-nineteenth century. One academic has gone so far as to call it 'a Lancashire dialect with an Irish accent',[21] but there were other influences on it as well. At the same time as the Irish, other immigrants from North Wales and Scotland were arriving in the city, and although Irish had by far the greatest influence, it was the interaction between the existing Lancashire dialect and the Irish, Scots and Welsh voices of the newcomers that produced today's accent. Another, less complimentary, description is 'a third Irish, a third Lancashire and a third catarrh'.

It is a highly localized accent, stretching only a little beyond Liverpool itself towards the M6 motorway, although there are traces of it in the speech of people in North Wales and even the Isle of Man—but because it's such a recent development, it's possible to see fairly clearly how it has grown up. The numbers alone suggest that the expansion of Liverpool during the mid-nineteenth century must have had some effect on the way English was spoken there: in the 1820s, '30s and '40s, the population more than trebled, from 119,000 to over 375,000. Census figures show that around 20 per cent of them were Irish-born, 5 per cent Welsh and 4 per cent Scottish. Many of these incomers would have spoken not English, but either Gaelic or Welsh as their first languages. And then there was the port, the largest in the British Empire, handling more than half the UK's trade, and bringing in people from all over the world to add their accents to this linguistic stew.

One feature of Scouse that may have developed from Irish English is the distinctive *r* sound, which is generally pronounced slightly further forward in the mouth in Liverpool than would be common elsewhere in Britain. The consonant is tapped with the tongue against the back of the front teeth or the alveolar ridge—the hard area just behind them—sounding somewhere between an *r* and a *d*. (The easiest way to find the alveolar ridge, by the way, is to pronounce the alveolar consonants, *d, l, n, s, t* and *z*, and let your tongue lead you to it.) That sort of *r* is a habit that is associated with fairly broad Scouse accents, and tends to come after *th* in words like *three* or *throttle*, or between vowels in words like *curry* and *berry*—although in

America, as we will see, it has become a clichéd way of representing British English.

But the most obvious habits that the Irish brought with them were the tendency to pronounce the vowel in the word *worse* the same as that in the word *scarce*, and also the distinctive pronunciation of *th*'s. It's usually written as a *t* or a *d*, as if the words *brother* or *thick* were pronounced *brudder* and *t'ick*, but in fact the consonant comes out somewhere between the two, with the tip of the tongue higher up in the mouth. As a result of that, the *t* sound itself can be pushed off the end of the tongue altogether, so to speak, so Cilla Black could promise her audience *a lorra, lorra laffs*. Similarly, at the end of the word, it can practically vanish, so that an attractive girl—or man, come to that, presumably—might be described as *fih* rather than *fit*, or maybe, if slightly less attractive, *all righ*. A similar thing happens with a *k* sound, which is produced further back in the throat, to get *snakh* or *breakh* rather than *snake* or *break*. A Merseysider who goes to buy a large box of deep-fried chicken from a fast-food store may watch the server *stikhen the chikhen in the bukheh*. There is a very similar back-of-the-throat consonant in Gaelic, which may have influenced the Scouse pronunciation—or maybe it is something that has grown up on its own. With so many different elements involved in the development of the accent, you can't

70

always point to a single cause-and-effect relationship of any one feature.

There are certainly elements of Scouse that are recognizably north-of-England—the flat *a*'s, for instance, the rounded *u* in *cup* or *brother*, or the lengthened *oo*-vowel in words like *book* or *look*. This was the accent that would have been common in Liverpool before the mass immigration of the mid-nineteenth century. But the actual voice production of Scouse seems to be unique—a development that has come from the mixture of different accents and ways of speaking. Some Liverpudlians put it down to the wind out of the Mersey Tunnel blowing up their noses, and outsiders often call it adenoidal, but the voice quality of a broad Scouse accent is different from any other English way of speaking. In fact, there are at least three distinct styles—some people speak with a half-swallowed, back-of-the-throat 'adenoidal' accent that sounds as if they have a bad cold, others with a very breathy production, and others—like the late John Lennon—in a very nasal style. It's not Ireland, and it's not north-of-England—it's Liverpool.

But Scouse isn't just an example of various different types of speech being thrown together to produce a new and distinctive accent. Listening to people talk on Merseyside is another reminder of how individual accents differ from one locality to the next, and how

71

they change over time. Phonologists have noticed recently that young Liverpudlians are starting to use pronunciations that might once have been more associated with London and the south-east, saying *fink* rather than *t'ink*, for instance, or *bruvver* instead of *brudder*. Nothing remains the same: trying to describe an accent on paper is like trying to nail smoke to a wall.

Different parts of Merseyside—St Helens, Widnes and Southport, for instance—have always had their own versions of the Liverpool accent. Even the four Beatles—probably in their day the most famous Scouse speakers in the world—all spoke differently. George Harrison had the broadest Scouse tones, Paul McCartney's were more restrained and middle-class, Ringo Starr's vowels were recognizably (at least to another Liverpudlian) from the traditionally Protestant area of Dingle, and John Lennon had the nasal twang which made self-important people think (usually rightly) that they were being sneered at. Again, few people from outside the city noticed the difference—for a time, in the US at least, the term 'Beatles accent' replaced 'Liverpool accent'. The radio disc-jockey John Peel, angling for a job in Texas in the 1960s, abandoned his public school voice for the phoney Liverpool accent that stayed with him for the rest of his life.

But the yeah-yeah-yeah years of The

Beatles, when Scouse was trendy and teenagers all over England practised their Liverpool vowels and their nasal sneer, are as distant now as winklepicker shoes and drainpipe trousers. Outside Merseyside, Scouse always comes near the bottom of lists that are drawn up to try to assess which regional accents are considered most 'desirable'. There is constant social pressure on anyone who leaves Liverpool to tone down a Scouse accent and also, as the teenagers saying *fink* and *bruvver* demonstrate, pressure on the accent from outside as well. Journalists, writing as if Scouse were a quaint survival of old England, warn periodically in the newspapers that it is likely to disappear altogether, drowned in a tide of *EastEnders* and south-eastern vowel sounds. But Scouse is a living, constantly changing way of speaking, not a museum exhibit. Accents are always under pressure: that's how they change and develop. And social pressure can work two ways as well: for every person whose accent mellows and retreats as he moves out of Merseyside, another stays at home and strengthens his Scouse accent in response to the perceived slights from outside. Those who predict the disappearance of regional accents like Scouse underestimate the strength of local pride.

Midlands accents also regularly rank around the bottom of national surveys of desirability—

a recent BBC poll, for instance, put the Birmingham accent at the bottom, with the Black Country only just above it. They are the accents of Jasper Carrott and Frank Skinner—the accent that could clearly be distinguished behind the carefully-enunciated voice of Enoch Powell. They are, as you might expect from a place at the crossroads of Britain, right on the border between rounded *u*'s and unrounded *u*'s or flat *a*'s and rounded *a*'s, the result of a mixture of influences from all over. There is an *eye* vowel in words like *make* or *face* similar to the one Cockneys use, while the vowel in words like *price* or *fine* becomes almost *oy*, and the *oh* in *no* or *slow* comes out as *ow*. And as for the *oo* sound in *goose* or *you*, no one who remembers Harry Enfield's objectionable wealthy Birmingham character who insisted on reminding everyone that he had *considerably more moonney than yee-ow* will need reminding about where that goes.

All these examples, of course, are simply caricatures: Harry Enfield is an impressionist, not a linguist. Even if they were written out in the phonetic script that no one but academics understands, they would still be approximations, an attempt to use an unchanging symbol to reproduce a sound that can vary considerably. But the important point about them is their sequence: as each vowel changes, it pushes the one next to it a little further along.

74

That change in vowel sounds seems likely to have started in London—probably well before the start of the nineteenth century, as the early convict settlers took it to Australia with them—but there are other aspects of the Midlands accents that clearly look to the north rather than the south. There are the *a*'s and *u*'s, of course, but also similarities to the back-of-the-throat pronunciation of Liverpool, and a Yorkshire-style difference between the vowels in *throat* and *stone*.

Why should those sounds be unpopular? It's partly, no doubt, because they're seen as an urban accent, but it's also mixed up with the whole question of preconceptions that we looked at earlier. These immediate, confident, and almost invariably wrong judgements we make about people from the way they speak aren't limited to the speech of the big cities. The one thing that everyone knows with absolute certainty, from listening to several of the characters in *The Archers* on Radio Four if nothing else, is that anyone who speaks with a West Country accent is necessarily an expert on agriculture, or possibly sails a small boat and wears a black eyepatch. This knowledge is taken out of the same drawer as the similar assumption that northern accents are the sole prerogative of people who work in factories that belch smoke, or that car dealers speak with either a Brummie or a Cockney accent, but it is surprisingly common. The late Liberal

MP David Penhaligon spoke with a broad Cornish accent all his life: but even though he was a talented and qualified mechanical engineer by training, who had made himself an expert in the problems of fishing, tin-mining and rural life which affected his Truro constituency, he used to joke with a slightly bitter edge about the way that people always wrote to him on farming matters, about which he knew next to nothing. And it wasn't only outsiders. Before being selected for the Truro constituency which he was to represent for twelve years until his death in 1986, Penhaligon was turned down for several other West Country seats, apparently partly because local party officials thought his accent would be unpopular.

One feature of Penhaligon's accent, like that of *The Archers* characters, was the so-called *rhotic r*, which was once universal across the country, and which crossed the Atlantic with the early settlers to help establish the American accent which survives to this day. What it means, simply, is that the *r* is pronounced in words like *farm* and *cart*. It's historic, sensible, and, especially when compared with the mish-mash of so-called standard English, extremely simple. Most English speakers have a fairly uneasy relationship with the letter *r*. Words like *start* and *square* practically lose their *r*'s when they are spoken, to become *staht* and *squay-uh*, while the final syllable of *father* or *mother* would be *-uh*, without the trace of an *r*. The *r* returns when the word is followed by a vowel, so that *father and mother* become *fathuh-rand mothuh*—but that happens too in phrases without a final *r*, so the name Emma would be pronounced *Emm-uh*, but *Emma and Becky* would be *Emmuh-rand Becky*.

But none of those complications is true in the west of England. If *u*'s and *a*'s mark a northerner, it is the letter *r* which reveals someone from the West Country. Among outsiders, it is often thought of as a rural accent, but it's prevalent too in big cities such as Bristol, Exeter, Southampton, Plymouth and Bournemouth, even with their mixed and cosmopolitan populations. It's only since the late seventeenth century that people elsewhere in England have started dropping their *r*'s, which explains why the rhotic *r* travelled to America but not to Australia, New Zealand or any of the colonies of the eighteenth century and later.

Another well-known aspect of the western accent in England is using *v* for *f*, *z* for *s*, and *zh* for *sh*, so that *farmer* becomes *varmer*, *supper* becomes *zupper*, and *ship* become *zhip*. Or so they say: the difference from the rhotic *r* is that you could travel the length and breadth of the region and hardly hear this pronunciation, which has virtually died out, except in the scripts of not-particularly-good comedians. It is likely that people from Somerset find hoary old remarks about *zoyder arpples from Zummerzet* about as funny as Yorkshire people find *ee bah gum*—another phrase which is written in the London papers but never spoken on the streets in Leeds.

One trick of pronunciation which does still survive, and which demonstrates one way in which accents develop, is the loss of a final *-l*, so that Bristolians will sometimes talk about *Bristow* rather than *Bristol*, and be admitted to *hospitow* rather than *hospital*. Bristol itself was originally called Bridgestowe, from the Anglo-Saxon *brycg-stow*, meaning the place of the bridge. In itself, it's not an uncommon urban trick of speech—Cockneys, if they really could ever bring themselves to eat jellied eels, would ask for *jewwied ee-uws*, and the habit has spread far beyond Bow Bells. It's probably caused by nothing more complicated than the fact that changing the *l* to a *w* can make sounding the word slightly easier—just try it, and you'll see that you can give your tongue a rest. Around the Bristol area, though, it has led to an over-correction in the local accent, so that people occasionally put *l*'s into words where they have no business. Just like the small boy looking in the *mirroh* because he thought *-er* sounded wrong, so Bristol seafarers are said to have travelled to *Australial*, a *comma* becomes a *commal*, and two teams on opposite ends of a rope have a

78

tuggle-war. One primary school teacher in Bristol was confused when one of her young pupils explained that he had missed school the day before because of his mother's illness. She had been suffering, he told her solemnly, because of her *dial-beetles*. It was only when the teacher mentally removed the intrusive *l*'s that she understood that the boy's mother had diabetes. Then there was the wealthy businessman who, innumerable philologists have noted gleefully, and not entirely convincingly,[22] had three daughters, whom he had christened Idle, Evil and Normal . . .

One book about the Bristol accent[23] reports a late-night conversation in a West Country bedroom. 'Smatter? Sony harp's too,' says the woman, sitting up in the middle of the night. 'Snow good. Eye muster got insomnial,' her husband replies as he gets out of bed. 'Eye shunt ave ad that tinner beans stray tafter tenner leaven pintser bit rail.' She shrugs her shoulders unsympathetically as she goes back to sleep. 'Gnat case, ice pecked yule have dire eel too,' she says.

The point is that the intrusive *l* has been going on for so long that it's no longer a mistake. It's become a part of the local accent, even though it is dying out now, so the girl who was learning to dance, and complained, 'I can rumble but I can't tangle,' would probably be misunderstood today. And of course, a West-countryman who wanted to be difficult might point out that not many people in Britain have completely sorted out how and when they should pronounce their *l*'s anyway. There's not much argument about *calf* and *half* or *talk* and *chalk*, for example, so we might come up with a rule that *a* and *l* together represent a vowel sound with no following *l* (though we would still not be sure whether that vowel sound was an *ah* as in *calf* or an *or* as in *talk*) but what about *almond*, or *talcum powder*? People argue about the first, but not about the second. And as for the name *Ralph*, we would only pronounce it *Rafe*, without the *l*, if we were being very British and wanted to sound particularly posh. (Americans, of course, would have no difficulty over *Ralph* with an *l*. Their only problem would be trying not to laugh at the cute British accent.) Or, on the other hand, what about *folk* or *yolk*, where we don't sound the *l*, and *polka* or *Colin*, where we do? That, of course, is before we get to *Malcolm*, where we both do and don't in quick succession, at which point we presumably throw up our hands in despair and abandon the whole pointless exercise.

If we were desperate to establish some kind of rule, we would have to start looking either at the other consonants in the word, or at the length of the vowel: a long *o*, as in *yolk*, seems to silence the *l*, while the short *o* of *polka* leaves it alone; a following *t*, as in *salt* or *Baltic*, seems to give it some protection, although it

80

changes the vowel sound from an *a* to an *o*. It does at least seem fairly clear that *without* a following *t*, the *l* in *al*-words is often silent— unless, of course, you count the words that come originally from Arabic, like *algebra*, *almanac* and *alcohol*. Or at least, it would be fairly clear if you also forgot about words like *pal*, *Dalmatian* or *halibut*. The rule, if it exists at all, is getting so convoluted and cumbersome that it gives us no help at all, a bit like a ruler made out of plasticine. Think about it too long, and you end up, like the Bristol businessman, sending birthday cards to Idle, Evil and Normal. And maybe one to their cousin, Monocle, as well.

*   *   *

Ask most people in the south-east of England, and they'll tell you they don't have an accent. It's not true of course, even though there is probably a higher proportion of prosperous middle-class families speaking various versions of Received Pronunciation in that particular corner of England than there is anywhere else in Britain. There has never been anything more U than money and power, and the wealthy and influential people living in the capital have always had an overwhelming influence on fashion, in speech as in everything else. Today, as we'll see in a later chapter, the non-U accent of the London working class is having its own effect in the wider world as an entire generation seems to swallow its *t*'s and pronounce its *l*'s as *w*'s— asking for a *li'uw bi' of miwk*, for instance.

Londoners sometimes claim to be able to tell which side of the river someone comes from, but no-one has ever described the distinction with any precision. Shaw was having fun: the differences in London voices are generally those of different classes and different immigrant groups. True Cockneys, the 'born within the sound of Bow Bells' lot, are every bit as snooty and exclusive about their lineage as any ermine-robed earl in the House of Lords—but their accent has spread over much of the East End of London. Ethnic Bengalis and Pakistanis in Brick Lane Market who have been brought up in the capital often sound like Alf Garnett when they speak, and Cockney, like any other regional accent, has a whole range of different degrees, in and out of London: just think of the cast of *EastEnders*.

In East Anglia, Bernard Matthews has made a fortune out of playing on his regional accent in advertising his 'bootiful' turkeys—and in fact, that particular habit of dropping the *y*-sound in *beauty*, *resume* or *music* is more widespread in Norfolk and Suffolk than anywhere else in the British Isles. Outside Norwich, East Anglia is also, with the north-east, one of the very few parts of England where *h*'s at the beginning of a word are quite safe. Even in day-to-day speech, there would be no confusion in rural East Anglia between *whose* and *ooze*, as there might be across the rest of the country. Instead, the two words that would sound the same would be *whose* and *Hughes*. For centuries, the region was isolated from the main thoroughfares across the country and the accent developed in its own way.

To the west of London, in counties such as Oxfordshire and Berkshire, you can hear some of the characteristics of West Country speech: the poet Pam Ayres, for instance, has made a point of retaining the glottal stop and the *oi* in *gra'ifoid*, (gratified) and the *ee-oo* in *fee-ood* (food) from her childhood in Berkshire such traditional rural accents still survive—in Kent, for instance, local people might claim to be able to tell a Kentishman, who lives to the west of the River Medway, from a man of Kent who lives to the east—but over the last couple of hundred years, the growth of cities all over Britain has spread urban accents in the areas around them. London, as the biggest city in the country, has simply been more powerful than most.

*   *   *

So regional accents have a history of their own. They are not in any sense a degraded form of some senior, 'authorized' form of the language—in fact, they often include features of spoken English that predate Received Pronunciation. What they don't generally have is respect. Alan Bennett complains in his diaries about the way his comments about the fall of Margaret Thatcher were reported in the *Guardian*. The paper printed what he said, but prefaced it with 'Oo 'eck,' and carefully dropped all his aitches. 'I suppose I should be grateful they didn't report me as saying, ' 'Ee bah gum, I'm reet glad t'Prime Minister's tekken 'er 'ook,' '" he noted bitterly.[24]

In any case, it will have occurred to many people reading this chapter that, while all the stuff about regional accents may be quite amusing, the problem is that it's just not true. In today's cosmopolitan world, we all know people from the West Country who don't sound as if they have just stepped out of *The Archers* studio. (Come to that, there are plenty of actors on *The Archers* who don't sound as if they had just stepped out of *The Archers* studio.) There are those who retain some aspects of their regional accent but modify others, so that many northerners treasure their flat *a*'s, but find their rounded *u*'s approaching closer and closer to a south-eastern *uh*. (I know they do, because I'm one of them.) Others say *bahth* and *cahstle*, and would sooner rip their tongue out with rusty pliers than rhyme *cut* with *put*. The Tory politician William Hague has a clear northern accent which was the delight of impressionists when he was Leader of the Opposition—but no one is ever going to mistake him for a Yorkshire miner. The giveaway *u* that he uses is not as rounded as a classic Yorkshire accent—if he says *cut*, it doesn't rhyme with *soot*. But it's not a fully-open southern *uh* either: Hague's vowels are a compromise, somewhere in between. Not only that, but inconvenient people like him, who speak with a regional accent but without a regional accent, are actually in the majority: traditional rural speech is dying out all over Britain.

Even so, the differences remain. A Leeds University academic called Stanley Ellis was called in by the police in the hunt for the Yorkshire Ripper in the late 1970s, after they received a tape recording from a man claiming to be the Ripper, who spoke with a broad north-east accent. They wanted Ellis, an expert on regional dialects and accents, to say where he came from. All they had was a few short sentences—'I'm Jack. I see you are still having no luck catching me,' the tape began, and went on to threaten to kill again in a chilling, expressionless monotone. For many old-school policemen, going to Ellis seemed to be the equivalent of turning to mystics with second sight—and they were astonished when he suggested not just Sunderland, but a small pit village on the outskirts of the town called Castletown.

The man who was eventually traced—nearly thirty years later—was a hoaxer, not the murderer. He lived less than one mile from Castletown. Ellis had used academic scholarship in developing a skill to match that of Shaw's Professor Higgins. Higgins' was an exaggeration, even in 1916—but Ellis proved that the principle was sound enough.

In the US—where, as we will see, regional and local differences have always been less marked than in the UK—a respected linguistics professor, Henry Lee Smith, starred in a 1940s national radio show called *Where Are You From?* in which he too performed much like Professor Higgins, telling whereabouts in the US contestants came from to within about fifty miles. Smith used a list of twenty key words, which he asked contestants to read aloud. The vowels in the words *marry*, *merry* and *Mary*, for instance, are all pronounced differently east of the Appalachian Mountains; to the west, the words are indistinguishable from each other. By cross-referencing a series of such geographical differences, Smith was able to narrow down the contestants' origins with remarkable success.

Ellis and Smith were both exceptional talents, but most people can still tell if someone with a regional accent comes from the north or the West Country; they can tell a Scotsman from an Irishman or a Welshman.

The vast majority of people retain at least some features of the local accents they grew up with, even years after they have moved to different parts of the country, and most of them can broaden their accents when they want to. Many do it unconsciously if they go home, or if they speak to people with more of a regional accent than their own. My own accent, dulled and emasculated by thirty years in the south of England, becomes rounder and fuller every time I travel back to Yorkshire; my children, all born in the south-east, fall about laughing when they hear me talking on the telephone to my brother in Wakefield.

Sometimes, this bilingualism in English can cause the same problems that foreigners experience when they are learning the language. If a northerner tries consciously to acquire a southern or RP pronunciation of his *u* vowels, he is likely to fall victim to Alan Bennett's 'incurable disease of the vowels'. Why is it *de rigueur* to have an open *u* in *but* but laughable to hear it in *butcher*? Obviously, the change from *put* with a rounded vowel to *putt* with a straight one is caused by the doubling of the consonant—but what about *but* and *butt*, where the sound doesn't change at all? And why do southerners say *pus* with an open vowel, but *Puss* with a rounded one? In fact, it's not so much a disease as a series of traps set by the written language into which our earnest northerner falls just as surely as

87

any foreigner learning English. If you don't pick up the language naturally, by copying the people around you—if you try to speak it logically, according to rules and spellings—it will turn around and bite you.

CHAPTER THREE

Ancient Languages
Welsh, Cornish, Scottish and Irish

The story of English is one of Anglo-Saxon merging with the French of the Norman conquerors after 1066, of Latin words grafted on to the language by scribes and scholars, and, later on, of foreign influences brought back by travellers, soldiers and traders. Many of the changes and innovations started in London and spread outwards throughout the rest of the country. Some took root in particular places and began to affect local speech; others didn't. With little direct contact between the various regions of the country, different dialects and pronunciations grew up, based mainly on the same Anglo-Saxon, French and Latin roots, with a mixture in some parts of the country of Viking languages from other generations of conquerors.

But more than a thousand years before the Anglo-Saxons, Celtic tribes had arrived in Britain, bringing their own Goidelic language with them from Central Europe. This developed into the various Gaelic languages spoken first in Ireland, Scotland and the Isle of Man, and then in Wales, Cornwall and Brittany in northern France. The old Celtic languages were pushed aside by Anglo-Saxon as it spread through England, but these versions survived for centuries—Welsh still thrives as an alternative to English—and have left behind their effect on the way English is spoken in these different parts of the country.

It used to be said that if you want to read the finest English of the last 150 years, then you have to go to the books of an Irishman—and preferably an Irishman who has left Ireland and gone to live in Paris. Bearing in mind Oscar Wilde, James Joyce and Samuel Beckett, there is just enough truth in the suggestion to annoy a lot of Englishmen, which many people might say was one good reason for making it. But it's certainly true that if you want to hear the finest English that has ever been spoken, then you have to listen to a Welshman.

That's my view, anyway—although it's only fair to add that not everyone agrees with it. In a BBC survey in 2005, Welsh was voted to be one of the least popular accents in the UK in terms of pleasantness and prestige, behind Northern Irish, Cornish and Australian. Swansea and Cardiff both came near the bottom of a list of accents which people felt might help a career, so presumably the poll was heavily influenced by the traditional dislike of urban voices. But as far as I'm concerned, whatever the BBC's voters said, the Welsh—probably in revenge for the way that English steamrollered their own tongue for generations—speak English like angels. They can take the language gallantly by the hand and dance with it, leading it to and fro, up and down, and relishing each word. Think of Richard Burton, of Dylan Thomas, of Catherine Zeta Jones, or Huw Edwards on the BBC Television News. In an earlier generation, there was the First World War prime minister David Lloyd George.

But then, it is not only, or even mainly, a question of the accent itself—none of the five I have mentioned has a particularly strong Welsh accent, and recordings of Lloyd George in particular show that he had actually adopted many of the mannerisms of the English upper classes in the way he spoke. In his speech on the Budget of 1909, for instance,[25] he talks about the *countreh*, the *Naveh*, and the *communiteh*. His political aims, he said with a politician's natural self-assuredness, would not be challenged *by any political party in the lend*. His native Welshness was more marked when he was angry or excited—but even in the relative calm of this speech, it is possible to hear the Welsh lilt of his sentences. Words like *smallholding* and *livestock* have the stresses equally balanced between the first and second syllables, rather than heavily on the first, as they would be with most Englishmen; a word like *co-operative* is practically spelt out, syllable by syllable.

In our own day, there is John Humphrys on Radio 4's *Today* programme. His accent, as he breakfasts on air over a freshly grilled and still-wriggling politician, might be taken practically as a new standard for BBC English. He has lived in London for over twenty years, but still has the hard, flat *a*'s, the breathy and slightly schoolmasterly *hw* to begin words like *what* and *where*, and the precise three-syllable pronunciation of words like *general*, that mark him out as the Cardiff boy he is. He most emphatically does not have a Welsh lilt. (I know that because he told me. His actual words were, 'If you say I have a Welsh lilt, I'll bloody kill you.' I think he was joking, but it just goes to show how strongly people feel about their own accents.)

But just as his accent has been affected by his time in England—though he'll probably kill me for saying that too—so it's unavoidable that the sounds of Welsh should be echoed in the English that is spoken in Wales. Until a couple of hundred years ago, the vast majority of people in the Principality spoke Welsh as their first language, and learned English—if they learned it at all—only to communicate with monoglot Englishmen. Even now, there are significant numbers of people who would describe English as their second language. Practically everybody can speak it, but maybe as many as a fifth of the population speak Welsh by choice, and learn their English at school.

This Welsh influence can sometimes be seen in the grammar—in the way, for instance, that a word may be dragged to the front of the sentence for emphasis. *Thirsty, I am*, a man might say as he walks up to the bar. Some sounds that are common in English, such as the *yu* sound in *few*, are not found at all in Welsh. Instead of *yu*, Welsh has a more distinct *ee-yu* which is carried over into English, so that *beauty* would be pronounced *bee-uwty*. The *t* in the middle of that word would also be a common mark of a Welsh accent, since consonants between vowels tend to be lengthened almost as though the speaker were sounding a double consonant. *Bee-uwt-tiful.* Welsh, a Welshman will tell you, is essentially a phonetic language, so that *education— edyucashun*, or even *edjucayshun* to most English speakers east of Offa's Dyke—might be pronounced *ediuwcaysh-iun*. Richard Burton, in his role as the journalist in the rock opera *The War of the Worlds*, had some elements of an English upper-class accent—he talked, for instance, about *the last years of the nineteenth centureh*, much as Lloyd George did before him—but he also paid that distinctive Welsh homage to the individual syllables. Earth was being watched, he said, *by minds immeasurably superior to ours*, and he drew out that word *immeasurably* with satisfaction. He hangs on the double-*m* sound as a classical

93

Latin speaker would do, and the central consonant is actually halfway between *zh* and *zu*, while the final *-ably* rolls around his mouth as if he is reluctant to let the syllables escape.

Or take the Master—Dylan Thomas himself—telling of his derring-do as a young big-game hunter in *A Child's Christmas in Wales*. 'We waited to snowball the cats. Sleek and long as jaguars, and horrible-whiskered, spitting and snarling, they would slide and sidle over the white back-garden walls, and the lynx-eyed hunters, Jim and I, fur-capped and moccasined trappers from Hudson Bay—off Mumbles Road—would hurl our deadly snowballs at the green of their eyes . . .'[26] He doesn't just read the words, he draws out their meaning with the sound of his voice. The long *s*'s sibilate softly in the background like the cats themselves; Thomas's breathy voice seems to taste the sounds of the words like whisky, capturing the *hw* of *whiskered* and *white*, and relishing the rapid tumble-downstairs dee-di-di of *horrible* and *moccasined*. Richard Burton and Dylan Thomas, of course, are not Everyman. They are the Yehudi Menuhins of the spoken word, with the advantages of deep, sonorous voices and, in Burton's case at least, years of training as a classical actor. Thomas's sound engineers make him sound as if he is speaking in a bathroom—and decades of whisky and cigarettes probably had something to do with the timbre of his voice as well. But

94

the delight of both men in the sounds of what they say, their respect for the individual syllables of the words themselves, echo in their voices.

A Welshman will roll the three syllables of *choc-o-late* around his mouth almost like—well—chocolate, while an Englishman will munch it down quickly in the two-syllable *choc-lut*, or maybe *choc-lu'*. There is also the double-*l* familiar from *Llanelli* or *Llanfairfechan*, which chokes most English people who try to pronounce it, and which is called a *voiceless alveolar lateral fricative*, a name which is almost as hard to say as the sound itself (I know I promised not to use academic jargon, but I couldn't resist that). And then, there is the simple, single *l* of words like *little*.

Simple? Well, not exactly, but it is a letter which separates not only Welsh from English, but also North Walians from South Walians. In standard English, there are two distinct pronunciations of *l*. Words like *follow* or *lettuce* have what is known as a *clear l*, with the tip of the tongue on the alveolar ridge, behind the front teeth, and the back of the tongue kept low; in words like *bell* or *film*, where the *l* is either at the end of the word or is followed by a consonant, the tip of the tongue still taps the alveolar ridge, but the back is raised towards the roof of the mouth in a *dark l*. A word like *little* or *label* has first one, then the other—just try it. So far, so simple—but in South Wales, most people use a clear *l* all the time, while in the north, they favour a dark *l*.

That *dark l* habit is part of a general tendency in North Wales to pronounce both vowels and consonants further back in the mouth—possibly due to the influence of Liverpool and the north-west of England, where it is also common. That's just one of many ways in which the speech of the neighbouring areas of England has affected both the Welsh and the English of Wales. Welsh has borrowed English words for centuries, for instance, generally preserving the sound, rather than the spelling. The Welsh word *gympass*, which means *around*, may make little sense to a non-Welsh speaker, until he realizes that the *y* is pronounced *oo* as in *foot*, and the word comes from *compass*. A more modern example would be *snwcer*, for *snooker*. Often, the borrowings can be disguised by the addition of Welsh plurals—bearing in mind the *u*-sound of the letter *y*, the word *jyg* is easy enough for an Englishman to understand as something he might put milk in—but *jygiau*, the plural, is more of a challenge. And of course, the exchange of words works in both directions: the Welsh phrase for a little dog, *cor gi*, has been translated into English to mean—well, a snappy little dog with a bad temper and royal pretensions.

Of course, there are local differences in the

sounds both of Welsh and English: the Welsh of North Wales is clearly distinct from that of the south, because the sparsely-populated central mountains have always proved a barrier to communication between the two areas. In the south, you can hear the influence of the West Country, and in the north, that of the Midlands. In most of Wales, for instance, the letter *r* is lost in words like *farm* or *cart*, much as it is across most of England—but along the borders of Gloucester, Hereford and Shropshire, the rustic west-of-England *r* of *farrm* or *carrt* is still common. And in Clywd, further north, the sounded final *g* of *ing* which makes *singer* rhyme with *finger* has clearly leaked across the border from the Midlands and the north-west. The influence of the way other people speak doesn't stop at national boundaries. Big cities, as we have seen already, have developed their own urban accents. The characteristic Cardiff *air* for *ar*, for instance, makes the name of the city sound like *Cairdiff* in a way which may seem oddly similar to the Scouse of Liverpool, until you remember that both cities are big ports with close connections to Ireland.

But even more important than the sound of the individual letters is the stress of words and sentences. In English, there is no hard and fast general rule about where stresses will fall, but in the Welsh language they frequently come on the penultimate syllable—a habit which carries over into the pronunciation of English words such as *eduCAtion* or *Por' TALbot*. There is also a tendency in Welsh English to concentrate on a single main stress in a word, whereas British English will often have a main stress and one or more secondary stresses—both an Englishman and a Welshman would say the word *econOMic*, for example, with the stress on the third syllable, but whereas an Englishman, whether he said *eh-con-omic* or *ee-con-omic*, would generally have a secondary stress on the first syllable as well, a Welshman would be more likely to give the first, second, and fourth syllables the same degree of stress. Those differences in stress, minor though they might seem, combine with the rising tone at the end of a sentence to give the language its distinctive lilting quality.

And what about the English in Wales? If the Welsh can waltz with the English language and make it sing, it's also true that the English have their own attitude towards Welsh. Whenever they come across it, either in official documents or in the Welsh place-names like Llanelli or Bancyfelin, they either ignore it, or they wrestle with it until they have their knee on its throat and they have choked it into submission. A couple of good friends were on a driving holiday in North Wales, and believed after a week or so that they had become passably competent at pronouncing the Welsh names they came across. One particular village kept cropping up on signposts so frequently that they decided to visit it. It was called, so far as they could pronounce it, something like *Boteghlithghars*, but it proved very hard to find. For several hours, they drove along narrow country lanes, following signs which seemed to keep sending them in different directions until eventually, tired and frustrated, they stopped and spelled out the word again in the gathering twilight. They looked this time with English eyes, rather than the Welsh eyes which they had tried so hard to acquire in order to improve their pronunciation of Welsh place-names. The letters on the signpost at the side of the road, which they had thought should be pronounced *Boteghlithghars*, were B-o-t-t-l-e-d g-a-s . . .

(It's entirely possible that this story might say more about my friends than about the Welsh language. On a later tour of Cornwall, after visiting the charming villages of St Merryn St Agnes and St Columb Major, they turned inland on a fruitless three-hour search for the well-signposted settlement of St Rawberries . . .)

*   *   *

The Celtic languages did survive for a while in England—but only just, hanging on by their fingertips to the Cornish peninsula. David

Penhaligon's rich Cornish accent, with its seemingly unending vowels and rolling cadences, was a legacy of the ancient language of Kernewek, which had practically vanished by the end of the eighteenth century after a long decline.

Like its close relative Welsh, or its more distant Gaelic cousins in Scotland and Ireland, Kernewek has left behind its shadow over the language that superseded it. It survives, predictably, in the names of people and of ancient communities—the old saying 'By Tre, Pol, and Pen you may know the Cornishmen' reflects the fact that *tre* meaning a town, *pol* meaning a pool or a body of water, and *pen*, a headland, are all Kernewek words which commonly turn up in place-names—but it also influences the way that English is spoken. The word *dhe*, for instance, meant both *at* and *to*, and some local speakers might say *to Truro* when a non-Cornishman would say *at Truro*. Similarly, it is a Cornish habit to use the word *how* when outsiders would use the word *why*— *How didn't you go to school today?* The word *belong* is used to express a habitual action, as in *I belong to do that*. There are distinctive word-orders as well: like the Welsh, a Cornishman might ask *Going to town are you?* All these are matters of grammar and syntax— but Kernewek lingers on, too, in the very sound of the Cornish voice.

The slow withdrawal of the language means

that its influence tends to be strongest in the far west. There are regional differences within Cornwall, but a few general points give a flavour of the accent and a sense of how it derives from the old language. Vowel sounds tend to be extended, so that words like *bath* or *bag* would have an *ah* sound that would be much longer than a conventional southern rounded *a*: the second vowel in *banana*, from a Cornishman, practically follows the curve of the fruit as it is dragged out. Some older speakers would make a distinction between *ee* and *ea*, so that *sea* would have a slightly more open *eh* sound; words like *boat* and *coat*, which a southern English pronunciation would give a simple *oh* vowel, might have an *oh-a* sound, reflecting the double vowel.

But the Cornish, unlike the more pernickety Welsh, are not precise about the pronunciation of each separate syllable. The Welshman picking lovingly over the five syllables of *co-operative* might be puzzled by the Cornish *c'wop'r'tive*. And as speech gets more colloquial, so whole words may be missed out or run together: *Going are you?*, already different from standard English, might be elided into *Goin' ar-ee?*

Many of these habits are increasingly restricted to older people. In Cornwall, as in other areas of England, the regional accent seems to be in retreat before the joint assault of incomers from other parts of the country, improved communications, and—the favourite villain—television. Many over-forties in Cornwall complain that teenagers sound as if they had just walked off the set of *EastEnders*. That is largely a matter of perception: London youngsters would be unlikely to think that those same teenagers were speaking with a London accent. The revival of the language which started in the early twentieth century still only affects a tiny minority of the population, but it is growing, and increased awareness of Kernewek may help the accent to remain. And in any case, saying that an accent is becoming less pronounced is not the same as saying that it's doomed. If the Anglo-Saxons of a thousand years ago are still remembered in the difference between the northern and southern *u*'s and *a*'s, then it seems likely that the descendants of the Celts who spoke Kernewek will continue to draw out their vowels and turn their sentences around for many years to come.

*   *   *

If a Welsh voice has more music and poetry than anybody else's, it is the Scots, and in particular the people of Inverness, who are traditionally known for speaking the most correct English. Leaving aside for the moment the question of what the word 'correct' means, and ignoring the cynical suggestion that the whole thing may simply have been an adroit public relations coup by some early native of Inverness—what is the reason for this enviable reputation?

It goes back to the dual roots of Scottish English. The Lowlands of Scotland were inhabited by Anglo-Saxons after they captured Edinburgh in the seventh century. They developed their own dialect of Old English, very similar to that of the people of Northumbria further south. As it gathered its own elements of Scandinavian and Norman French, this way of speaking spread across southern and parts of eastern Scotland. It was known originally—and a bit confusingly—as Inglis, until in the fifteenth century, when it had become the official language of the Scottish court, it was renamed Scottis or Scots. At that time, it enjoyed a flourishing literary tradition, with poets like Dunbar and Douglas, but from the sixteenth century onwards, the status of the language gradually declined. There was no Scots translation of the Bible, for instance, so the language of religion became the English of the King James version; the Act of Union in 1707 meant that the language of government, too, became the English of England. It became a matter of honour for a Scot with any social ambition to be able to write and speak in southern English, so that Dr Johnson was coming as close as he ever did to a compliment when he told his faithful Boswell that he considered him 'the most unScottified of your countrymen.' Robbie Burns wrote poetry in Scots—but at the same time, he also wrote fluently both in English and also in a sort of 'Scots-lite' which featured Scottish words and phrases, but which would have been easily understood by an English audience.

Further north in Scotland, Anglo-Saxon never arrived at all. Across the Highlands, people spoke Scottish Gaelic for centuries, a completely separate language which, as we have seen, developed from the Goidelic language of the Celts. When English was introduced as the language of government and official life with the Act of Union at the start of the eighteenth century, it had to be learned as a completely foreign language, so it was spoken without any of the habits of Lowland Scots speakers. Inverness was by far the biggest city in the Highlands—and so the social elite there became known as the most accomplished speakers of 'correct', or southern, English.

Whether Scots is a dialect of English or a separate language in its own right is the sort of argument that can go on for ever, and will probably involve you in fisticuffs at some stage. For those who care about official pieces of paper, it is listed in the European Charter for Regional or Minority Languages, and it is certainly true that much of Henryson's and

Dunbar's poetry can be understood only with difficulty by a southern English speaker. It's also true that it has won the contest with Gaelic. Today, there are very few native speakers of Gaelic, and the numbers are falling, but many people in Scotland switch easily between the vocabulary and grammar of Scots and those of English with a Scottish accent. For most people south of the border, knowledge of Scots would be limited to a once-a-year slurred version of *Auld Lang Syne*, but in Scotland itself, it provides a distinctive and ancient vocabulary. *Outwith* for *outside* would be one example of a Scots word that has never been adopted elsewhere, *pinkie* for little finger another—although that is also common in the US—or *greet* for *weep*—I remember a Scottish friend telling a colleague who had become tired and emotional after a long night in the bar, 'Dinna greet, mon.' Scots, like Welsh, also has a guttural *kh* sound, as in *dochtir* (daughter), which comes directly from Gaelic and is only found south of the border in the few words that have been borrowed from the language, such as *loch*.

It's still true that in Scotland, as in every other region of the British Isles, there are different accents of English in different areas. One study of Scottish dialects quotes a man from Fife saying to an Aberdonian, 'Onywye, we're no' the fowk that caas *fush* feesh.' (*Anyway, we're not the folk that calls fish*

105

'feesh'.)[27] The cut-glass tones of Edinburgh Morningside, where it's said that sex is what the coalman delivers the coal in, are very different from the broad Glasgow accent of Billy Connolly, and different again from the softer voice of someone from the Isle of Skye. The Speaker of the House of Commons, Michael Martin, has a broad Glaswegian accent which led some MPs to refer to him as 'Gorbals Mick'—a nickname which others pointed out was not only rude, but also inaccurate, since he came not from the Gorbals area of Glasgow, but from nearby Anderston, the same part of the city where Billy Connolly spent his childhood.

But there are still features which characterize the pronunciation of Scottish English as a whole. Like the Geordies of north-eastern England, for example, the Scots have no habit of dropping their initial *h*'s, so that there is always a clear distinction between the *Highlands* and *Islands*. One of the most noticeable features is the lack of the short *oo* sound that most English speakers would use in *foot* or *soot*. A Scotsman would use the same vowel sound in those words as he would in *goose*—and, like the flat *a* of a Yorkshireman, the habit is often one of the last to be eradicated when he moves south. The only other places where it is found are in Northern Ireland and northern parts of Northumberland, where there has been a clear

Scottish influence.

The Scottish *r*, of course, is pronounced wherever it is written. That's why no one in Scotland would get the words *fought* and *fort* mixed up; and for many speakers, *world* would have two syllables and *cart* might sound similar to *carrot*. George Galloway, the Respect Party MP who rejoices in the nickname Gorgeous George because of his natty suits, phallic cigars and cultured Dundee accent—he is probably the only person in the world who doesn't realize that the nickname is ironic— told one of the other contestants in the *Big Brother* programme on television that she was a *wickud perrson*. The first vowel of *person* was closer than it might have been in a rural Scottish speaker, who might have said *pairrson*, but Galloway retained both the *uh* sound of the second syllable of *wicked*, where most Southern English speakers would say *wickid*, and also the Scottish *r*, pronounced by tapping the tongue on the bony ridge behind the front teeth. Those Scottish vowels are responsible for the well-worn joke about the Edinburgh lady sitting down to tea. 'Is that a cake or a meringue?' she asks. 'No, you're quite right, it's a cake,' comes the reply.

Over the last few decades though, that traditional Scottish rolled *r* in the middle of *meringue* and at the start of *wrong* has become less common. As early as the beginning of the twentieth century, phonologists were noting

107

that rolled *r*'s were becoming less noticeable, and a study in the 1930s suggested that even then, only three Scottish students out of ten habitually rolled their *r*'s.[28] It is still a habit which often recurs when a speaker is angry or agitated in some way: I once saw a Scottish journalist from the Isle of Bute, where, he told me, you can tell if it's going to rain because you can see the mainland—if you can't see the mainland, then it's raining already—explaining why he would not drink with a particular politician at Westminster, 'Because he's *corrrrupt*,' he snarled, as he turned away.

There are also differences across Scotland in the way that the *ur* in *bird*, *herd*, and *curd* is pronounced. Some areas make a distinction between them—in the Highlands, for instance, *er* would be pronounced with an *air* sound, so James Naughtie, the BBC's *Today* programme presenter, who comes from the town of Huntly in Aberdeenshire, regularly describes himself as being *sairrtin* rather than *certain* that something or other is the case. In fact, he goes further, and tends to pronounce the second syllable of *appearance* as *air* as well, so that when he speaks about *the parents* of somebody, it is only the context that makes clear that he is not talking about their *appearance*.

It would be a brave man who suggested that Scots Gaelic was actually dead: languages inspire passionate loyalty, and the 2001 census showed 58,652 respondents still describing themselves as Gaelic speakers. But in the ten years since the previous census, that figure had fallen by over 10 per cent; there is now nowhere where only Gaelic is spoken; and the vast majority of the few people who speak the language at all live in the remote Western Isles. There is no sign of a resurgence of Gaelic to match that of Welsh.

But languages leave footprints behind them—*whisky* is short for the Gaelic word meaning *water of life*, although the Gaelic spelling *uisgebeatha* might seem less familiar— and the speech of the ancient Celts echoes in the English that is spoken where it is still remembered. Across the sea in Northern Ireland, the poet Seamus Heaney, for instance, in the introduction to his modern version of *Beowulf*, describes how he stumbled upon the word *lachtar* in an Irish dictionary, and recognized the familiar expression which his English-speaking aunt had used all her life to describe a flock of chickens. I had a similar moment of linguistic ecstasy when I first heard the Swedish word *fartlek*—an expression which is guaranteed to make small boys snigger, and which refers to a form of athletics training in which you walk and run at various speeds. It translates, a woman in the Swedish Chamber of Commerce told me, as *speed-play*. The Swedish word *lek*, then, pronounced *lehk*, means *play*—and exactly the same word is used in Yorkshire as a dialect expression meaning—

yes, you guessed it—*play*. Hiding there, in the way people speak today, is a memory of how the Viking ancestors of my Chamber of Commerce friend used to come over more than a thousand years ago to knock hell out of my own longsuffering forebears.

The same thing happens with the pronunciation of different words. Gaelic has no *z, zh* or *j* sounds, so that in the Western Isles, the *s* in words like *houses* or *islands* would be pronounced with a softer, *s*-sound—*houssess* and *islandss*. The *zh* in the middle of *measure* would be *sh*, and the word *janitor* would be pronounced *chanitor*. Similarly, Gaelic makes little distinction between *p* and *b, t* and *d*, or *k* and *g*, so *butter* might sound to an outsider like *putter, indeed* like *inteet*, or *goal* like *coal*. Another Gaelic habit which has spread into the pronunciation of English, both in Western Scotland and in Ireland, is the insertion of a brief vowel sound between two consonants, which results in characteristic pronunciations like *fillum* for *film* or *gurrul* for *girl*.

But the one fact that any non-Scot forgets at his peril is that Scotland is a nation, not a region. Across the rest of Britain, as we've seen, regional accents become less marked the higher up the social scale you climb, so that it becomes harder and harder to tell where a person was born by the sound of his voice—Received Pronunciation, the English of the BBC and the Boardroom, is generally accepted in England as a standard form of the language that offers no clue to geographical origins. It's true that even in Scotland, public schools often turn out pupils who speak RP English with barely a hint of a Scottish accent, and that Caledonian Societies of expatriate Scots all over the country can often sound, as one Scottish friend told me, like meetings of Surrey stockbrokers—but Scotland has its own prestige accent, which fills much the same role as RP does south of the border.

Scottish Standard English, as it is generally known, is as different from a working-class Glaswegian accent as RP is from Cockney—but it is still identifiably Scottish. Like RP in England, it is essentially the language as spoken by educated urban middle-class people. The letter *r* may be pronounced less emphatically than it would be in Glasgow, but it is still clearly different from most accents of English: whereas most accents south of the border would make no distinction between *paws* and *pores* or *cawed* and *cord*, they would sound quite different in Scottish Standard English. There are individual words that may be pronounced differently as well—*tortoyz*, for instance, instead of the English *tortus*, like Lewis Carroll's 'We called him Tortoise because he taught us', or *with* with a soft final *th* as in *thin*, rather than the voiced *th* of *though* or *that* which an Englishman would use.

But the important thing about Scottish Standard English is its essential similarity to RP: the two accents have the same role. Just as RP provides a way of speaking in England which disguises a person's geographical origins, but demonstrates a degree of education and social standing, so Scottish Standard English performs the same function in Scotland. There would probably be slight differences in the way that a middle-class, educated person from the Western Isles, an Aberdonian, or a Lowlander might speak Scottish Standard English, but the immediate message that their accent would give a listener would be about their social class rather than where they came from.

*   *   *

All the languages of the Celts have left their marks on English as they have succumbed—occasional words, grammatical structures, and pronunciations that echo the old Celtic way of speaking. In Ireland, though, the situation is different: for a time, at least, it was English, not Gaelic, that was under pressure and likely to disappear. In Ireland, unlike Wales or Scotland, English was for a time a language facing extinction. The language had been spoken there at least since the thirteenth century—the British Museum has a manuscript from that date which includes sixteen poems written in a dialect of English which would have been very similar to that of south-west England—but less than four hundred years later, it had virtually died out. The 'planters' who shipped over from England as colonists in a new wave of immigration during the seventeenth century took their language with them, but for at least a hundred years, English remained at risk of vanishing. It was only in the nineteenth century, after the Act of Union with Great Britain, that it really took hold—it is estimated that in 1800 at least half the population of Ireland spoke Irish, but within fifty years, that proportion had shrunk to about a quarter, with only around 5 per cent having no knowledge of English.

It is generally when languages are confident and expanding that they change and develop: Welsh, for instance, has blossomed with new words in the thirty years since the revival of the language started. When they are under threat, like English was in Ireland, they tend to avoid change and become very conservative. Several features of Irish English as it is spoken today reflect this.

Words like *which* and *whine*, for instance, had in most accents of British English lost the sound of the *h* they retain in their spelling by the middle of the eighteenth century. Certainly today, over most of the British Isles, it is impossible to tell simply from the sound whether a speaker is saying *whine* or *wine*, or

113

which or *witch*. In Scotland and Ireland, however, the *h* simply never went away. In most of England, the pronunciation *hwen* for *when* would sound purist and over-correct, but when Bob Geldof—not often accused of being pernickety or over-correct—says *hwen hwere* and *hwether*,[29] it is barely noticed, because the words fit so perfectly with his Dublin accent.

Similarly, British English began to shorten the final syllables of words like *secretary*, *seminary*, and *monetary* around the beginning of the seventeenth century. Other words, like *ceremony*, *category* and *strawberry* began to change around the same time, so that today, most British English speakers would say *secret'ry*, *semin'ry*, *monet'ry*, *cerem'ny categ'ry* and *strawb'ry*. If you do well in your exams, you may be presented with a *stiff-cut* rather than a certificate. The change came too late to affect American English, which still spells out each syllable—and it also left Irish English unaffected.

The same applies to the rhotic *r*—the *r* pronounced in words like *form* or *barn*. British English, outside the south-west, lost it, so most accents would now say *fahm* and *bahn*, while Ireland, like Scotland and most of North America, still keeps it. When writers try and create an Irish accent on the page, one of the favourite words they use is *sorr*, for *sir*. But the most striking example of English surviving unchanged over the centuries is the vowel

114

in words like *leaf* or *meat*, which in Middle English, before the Great Vowel Shift of the fifteenth century, would have been pronounced with an open *ay*—much as it is in rural Irish English today.

So the English roots of modern Irish English are unaffected by many of the changes that have taken place in the language in England itself over the last few hundred years. But in Ireland, just as in Wales and Scotland, the old Celtic language has been exerting its influence as well. Occasionally, Gaelic words slipped quietly across the border to take up residence in English—*trousers*, for instance, comes from the Gaelic word *triubhas*—but it is in the place names that the language can be seen most clearly. The novelist Brigid Brophy gave a graphic taste of how it sounds in a short poem in which she rhymed *Dun Laoghaire* with *draoghaire* (her imitation-Gaelic spelling for dreary) and *Drogheda* with *avoghed a* (avoid a).**30**

Of course, you can do the same thing in many languages—and it is hard for a speaker of English to mock other people's bizarre and illogical spellings and pronunciations. Consider the sad story of a young man travelling around England with his girlfriend:

> *I thought she was ghame*
> *in Thame;*
> *I bleicester*

115

In Leicester
And kicester
In Bicester—
But I loucester
In Gloucester.

But Brigid Brophy's rhymes are a useful reminder of the way that Irish Gaelic, or Erse, still colours the language of Ireland. Place names are always going to reflect linguistic history—think of the Viking settlements in England which grew into Skipton and Scunthorpe, or the Saxon towns of Peterborough and Hastings—but the way the Celts spoke still echoes too in today's daily language of the Irish. For example, Gaelic has no simple equivalent for the English words *yes* and *no*, so that the only way to answer a direct question would be to repeat the verb: *Are you coming? I am.* It is a habit which is often carried over into Irish English, commonly with the addition of *that* for emphasis.

One way in which the pronunciation of Gaelic differs from most accents of English is that the letters *t* and *d*, which in English are generally made with the tongue against the bony ridge behind the front teeth, are made instead against the teeth themselves. This tends to make a more breathy sound, which brings together *t* and *th* as in *thin*, and also *d* and *th* as in *though*, leading to the stereotypical representation of an Irish accent with phrases

116

like *tirty-tree* or *I'll be betther afther a dhrink.* This example, though, shows how dangerous it is to rely on stereotypes to describe an accent, partly because the mergers of *t, d* and *th* are certainly not universal across Ireland, and partly because there generally is a slight difference between, for instance, the words *tin* and *thin* in an Irish accent. Anyone who isn't used to hearing Irish English may fail to pick it up, but though the sounds are closer together than they would be in other accents of English, the distinction is there.

Stereotypes, however unreliable they may be, do sometimes reveal something—even if, as in this case, it's only the thick ears—or perhaps that should be the *t'ick ears*—of the English, but they are fraught with danger. On the stage and in books, Irishmen are often presented as sounding the *eye* vowel as a rounded *oi*, so that they would say, for instance, *Oi'm having a noice toime.* Englishmen see the writing, and when they hear the sound, they imagine it as an *oi* sound as in *boil* or *spoil*—but as soon as you listen to an Irish voice, you realize that the *oi* habit is really very rare. A few speakers from the rural and southern areas of the country may come close to a rounded *oi*, but for the vast majority, all that happens is that the sound begins slightly further back in the mouth. (Much the same is true of the similar vowel sound that is a characteristic of south-western speech in

England as far east as Oxfordshire.)

Oi may be the closest that letters can get to it, but it is a very inaccurate representation of what is actually in most cases simply a slightly more open *eye* sound: in this case, what the stereotype demonstrates is not only the failure of people to listen to the sound of what is said, but also the inadequacy of the alphabet.

It does, though, focus attention in passing on one historical quirk of the language—the confusion that existed for centuries in England as well as in Ireland between the *eye* and *oi* sounds. It wasn't until the nineteenth century that words like *join*, *oil*, *boil* and *poison* finally settled with an *oi* vowel, and in fact many of them are still pronounced with an *eye* in some dialects. It also demonstrates how stereotypes, or attempts to capture an accent in idiosyncratic spelling, can affect the way that sounds are actually heard.

But people have been mimicking Irish and other accents for centuries. Shakespeare had a very non-PC full hand of comic Irishman, Scotsman and Welshman in *Henry V*, with the king's soldiers Macmorris, Captain Jamy and Fluellen. (He might be spared prosecution, because he's not particularly kind to the English in this play either, with Pistol, Nym and Bardolph.) 'By Chrish, la, tish ill done!' Macmorris says. 'The work ish give over, the trompet sound the retreat.' Shakespeare is as good as most writers at representing spoken

118

accents on the written page—which is to say, not very good at all. But Macmorris's speech does catch the Irish habit of pronouncing *t*'s very softly and breathily, and it suggests the rounded, northern-style *u* of *trumpet*. Later on, he declares that 'the town is beseech'd,' reflecting the softer Irish *g*. What Shakespeare is doing, like all writers trying to reproduce non-standard accents, is picking a few characteristics, exaggerating them, and bundling them together in an attempt to catch the flavour of the spoken word. It need not be malicious—the three soldiers are presented as brave and loyal followers of King Henry—but it is very rare for anyone to see his own accent represented on the page and to feel that it has been well done.

One danger of placing too much reliance on stereotypes is fairly obvious: sit in a Dublin bar and throw together a few attempted examples of what you remember as the characteristics of an Irish accent, and you will very likely offend people and get yourself a well-deserved punch on the nose. But there is another danger: fail to listen properly to an Irishman like Bob Geldof or Fergal Keane, and you will miss hearing how the different elements of the stereotype, mellowed and varied, fit together into a subtle, expressive, and almost musical accent. Language grows up with us from childhood: it is part of us, like our face or our character, and without a trace of where we come from, it can be as unexciting and bland as a supermarket lettuce.

In the north of Ireland, the situation becomes even more complex. As the language developed, the same influences of seventeenth-century English and Gaelic were at play, but with the added complication of a huge influx of Scottish settlers—and even the Gaelic and English elements of the mix were different from those in the south. From as early as the thirteenth century, there were close links and frequent exchanges of population between western Scotland and Ulster, with Gaelic-speaking mercenaries, settlers and adventurers moving across the Irish Sea in both directions. In those days, Ulster consisted of the six counties of Antrim, Armagh, Down, Fermanagh, Londonderry and Tyrone, which today make up the province of Northern Ireland, plus the three counties of Donegal, Monaghan and Cavan which are now in the Republic. The accent in these three counties still has generally more in common with Northern Ireland than with the rest of the south.

At the same time, the Gaelic language itself had been affected, so that the Gaelic of Donegal—the only part of Ulster where the language survives—remains strikingly similar to Scots Gaelic and different from that spoken elsewhere in Ireland. So the Gaelic thread of the history of the Ulster accent leads off in a different direction—and so too does the English. Most of the Englishmen who established plantations around the Dublin area in the south during the sixteenth century were West-countrymen, but the vast majority who travelled to Ulster were from the north and the west Midlands of England. Add in the Scots planters who travelled to the province, taking their own Scots dialect and accent with them—and it is no surprise that the Northern Irish accent is so different from that of the south. There was little contact between the two English-speaking enclaves for at least a century—a belt of Gaelic-speaking Irish separated them from each other in the same way that the Welsh hills kept the people of north and south Wales apart, so that they developed in their own directions until today, the linguistic divide is at least as great as that over religion or politics.

One of the most obvious features of the Ulster accent in both parts of the province—and a clear inheritance from its Scottish roots—is the way that words like *foot* and *root* are pronounced with the same long vowel sound. Other vowels, too, are often lengthened much as they are in Scotland, so that *men* would become almost *meh-un*, or *great* would be *greh-ut*—think of John Cole and 'the scree-ut Prime Minister.' The Ulster pronunciation of a short *i* would generally be more like *uh*, so the late Social Democratic Party politician was

121

known as *Gerry Futt* rather than *Gerry Fitt*. If you wanted a kipper for your breakfast, you might be offered a *kupper*. (Although you would be mad to ask for one, because the Ulster Fry, a mountainous pile of everything you could imagine that could possibly be fried for breakfast—except kippers—is one of the great wonders of the gastronomic world. It is also, it should be added, probably the equivalent of six separate heart attacks on one plate.)

But then, as if to demonstrate that Ulstermen can sound their vowels as pedantically as anyone, you come to words like *Birmingham*, *Oxford* and *workman*, where most accents of British English would lose the vowel of the final syllable in a weak little *uh*. In Ulster, as in the United States, those final syllables would be pronounced clearly—*Birming-hahm*, *Ox-ford*, and *work-mahn*.

One of the most noticeable features of the consonants in the Ulster accent is the way that *t*'s are often pronounced as *d* when they come between two vowels, in much the same way as they are in America: Protestants are known as *Prods*, not *Prots*, and *matter* would sound like *madder*. *R* sounds are generally pronounced, as they would be in both southern Ireland and Scotland: imagine Ian Paisley rolling his way through the four syllables of *No surrrrenderrrr*.

*   *   *

The BBC poll that so damned the Welsh accent was one of many over recent decades which have arranged regional accents in order of how pleasant, prestigious, or socially desirable they are. A similar survey, carried out a few months later, reached much the same conclusions, with the added twist that Welsh found itself languishing around the bottom of a list of accents which supposedly gave the impression of hard work and diligence. It is significant that of the ten accents at the bottom of the poll, seven were those of big industrial cities or conurbations, namely Bristol, Swansea, Manchester, Glasgow, Liverpool, Black Country and Birmingham. There are other fairly clear prejudices against the other three, South African, German and Asian—but overall, the poll was simply a vote against urban working-class speech. It is probably not unduly cynical to point out that the second survey was carried out on behalf of the Aziz Corporation, a company which specializes in 'executive communications', and includes 'voice development' among the services it offers. It's also noticeable that surveys such as these tend to take place either in summer or around Christmas, when news is in short supply.

In any case, of course, such judgements of pleasantness or diligence based on the way people pronounce their vowels are entirely subjective—similar surveys in the past have also suggested that people imagine RP-speakers to be better-looking, cleaner and even taller, which goes to show how sensible the surveys are. Several phonologists have pointed out that when people describe the Cockney pronunciation of the word *paint* as 'ugly', they seem to have no objection when exactly the same pronunciation is used in Standard English for *pint*. The sounds of words are just that—sounds. In themselves, they are neither ugly nor beautiful.

It may or may not be true that the accent with which a person speaks can be a handicap in professional or social life, but what certainly *is* true is that people believe it is. Since that is the case, and since we know that it is possible for people to modify or reduce their accents, why do regional accents survive at all? If it is so clearly in their interests, then why don't people all speak with the Received Pronunciation accent which habitually tops the polls?

To a certain extent, accents *have* changed. The broad traditional regional accents are much less common than they were fifty years ago, and increasing numbers of people retain only an echo of the way their grandparents spoke. But the vast majority of people *do* retain that echo: relatively few want to cut themselves off entirely from their roots.

After reporting the conclusion that Welsh

was one of the most unpopular accents, the BBC pollsters then went on to question Welsh people themselves, and found that 56 per cent of them were proud of the way they spoke and had no desire to change. In an earlier experiment, researchers had measured the accents of Welsh interviewees electronically, and then asked them—in meticulously 'correct' RP English—why they bothered with a language like Welsh which, they said, had no use and no future. In every case, as the interviewees grew more annoyed—just as the researchers had intended—their accents became stronger. In those two findings, perhaps, lies the key to why regional accents survive in the modern world.

For everyone who wants to hide where they came from, there are many more who are proud of their origins, and when they get angry and speak more passionately and more instinctively, that pride shows in their accent. Regional accents, in any case, are often associated with positive qualities—in Thomas Hardy's novels, for instance, a rural Wessex accent is generally a mark of honesty and solidity. And would you rather be Lady Chatterley's lover, Mellors, with his broad Derbyshire accent, or her grand and cuckolded husband, Sir Clifford? There have always been jokes about the way people speak—but regional accents come off best at least as often as they are the butt of the humour.

There is the Edinburgh lawyer, for instance, who summoned the waiter to ask him condescendingly with carefully enunciated Standard Scottish vowels, 'What's the *soupe du jour*?' The waiter—inevitably, a Glaswegian—paused for a moment before replying, in his most guttural, working-class 'Weegie', 'It's the soup of the day'.

Or there's the Londoner who draws to a halt in his Rolls-Royce in the Yorkshire town of Pudsey. 'I say, my man, why did they build Pudsey railway station so far from the town centre?' he asks. The Yorkshireman pauses and scratches his head. 'We-e-e-ll,' he says at last, in his ponderous northern accent, ' 'appen they wanted to put it by t'trehns.' And in that word *trehns* rather than *trains* was all the centuries-old contempt of the provinces for the capital city.

The more conscious people are of their identity as a separate community, the keener they are to retain the links with it that their accent offers: Oliver Mellors used his accent to identify with the working people of Derbyshire, and to distinguish himself from the middle-class world of the Chatterleys. But a sense of nationhood gives even more strength to this feeling of community loyalty. For many Welsh and Scots, for example, being different from London or England is important for its own sake: their awareness of their status as members of separate nations, with separate histories and traditions, is echoed in their voices. The way we speak says who we are—and we want people to know it.

CHAPTER FOUR

New Accents of English
Asian and Black influences

My first tentative steps towards learning how to speak French were taken at the age of 10, under the guidance of a woman who had all the spark and imagination of a block of wood. For lesson after lesson—that's the way it seems now, looking back after more than forty years—the whole class sat chanting vowel sounds from a list of incomprehensible symbols chalked on the board. I didn't know then that she was using the International Phonetic Alphabet, and I don't suppose I would have cared. A Frenchman walking in on this roomful of unhappy children would have been bemused to hear that they were learning the language of Voltaire and Flaubert, and I sometimes wonder now whether the teacher was actually an early Europhobe, cunningly dedicated to inspiring the class with a passionate loathing for France and all things French.

Fortunately, at a new school a year later, another, more enlightened teacher took over. His way of demonstrating to us that the sounds of one language differ from those of another was to explain that, while the Scots roll their *r*'s by vibrating their tongues (a knack that eludes me to this day) the French used the little flap of skin at the back of the mouth called the uvula. Our first homework was to stand in front of the mirror after brushing our teeth at night and make a rolling French *r*-sound by vibrating our uvulas. It was not an easy task—I couldn't get it right for some time, and my parents thought I was being sick—but, being something of a swot, I persevered. The lesson I learned was that, tricky as it was, it was possible. My uvula was the same as that of a Frenchman—I simply had to learn to use it properly. (The new skill had unexpected benefits: apart from pronouncing *r* in French, I can now join in fairly creditably with Roy Orbison's growl of delight in *Pretty Woman*.)

The differences in pronunciation between languages are the source of limitless jokes—Arabic makes no distinction between *b* and *p*, and even Arabs who speak excellent English may frequently refer to the 'pumpers' on their car, or the 'bassbort' which they have to produce for immigration officials. A young, blonde and beautiful colleague called Penny Berry who used to read the news on Dubai Television, found herself regularly being introduced on air as Benny Perry. There may, too, be difficulties over recognizing particular abbreviations, as the Qatar Television announcer giving the result of the FA Cup found out: 'And in the English fuck-up . . .' he started off solemnly.

The problems are not all one way, as any English speaker who has tried to reproduce *'ayn*, the initial Arabic vowel sound of *'Ali*, will know. (For the record, you make as flat a northern *a* as you can imagine, then flatten it further and swallow it as far back in your throat as you can manage without choking.) Consonants, too, are traps for the unwary: I once startled a friend when I tried to compliment him on his big heart, and inadvertently told him instead that he had a big dog. After looking round in puzzlement for this Arab Hound of the Baskervilles, he showed me patiently how I had confused the words *qelb* and *kelb*. At first, they sounded identical to me—it was only later that I learned that the *q* should have come from further back in my throat until it sounded like a throttled *g*.

The point is that the physical act of producing a particular sound can be learned— we all have the same basic biological equipment, and it is only lack of practice that makes the clicks that feature in several African languages, the French *r*, or the Arabic *'ayn* hard for an English speaker to master. More than that, it is only habit that makes us distinguish between one pair of sounds and not another: there are different types of *k* in English just as there are in Arabic (just try saying *keel*, *cull* and *cool*, and listen to the initial sound of each word), but because they don't affect the meaning, an English speaker will not notice them. An Arab, on the other hand, will find it hard to tell *p* from *b*, because his own language makes no distinction.

Such habits not only *can* be learned, but they *are* learned. Mass immigration into Britain over the last sixty years brought hundreds of thousands of families into the country from the Indian subcontinent, many of whom spoke little or no English. In some cases, particularly among women who seldom left their houses to mix with the local population, they never learned, and many of those who did pick up English after they arrived retained pronunciations and speech patterns from the languages they had learned as children, sometimes making what they said more or less unintelligible to local people. Parts of many British cities became largely foreign-speaking areas.

Among the next generation, however, which grew up in Britain, the change was remarkable. Young men and women learned and spoke English literally like natives as they grew up— not the formal Received Pronunciation of the textbook, but the locally flavoured language of the cities where they lived. Whether they thought of themselves as British, British Indian or British Pakistani, the accents in which they spoke were often indistinguishable from those of their white contemporaries. The boxer Amir Khan, talking to reporters on television after winning his silver medal in the Athens Olympics, had a broad Lancashire accent which was very different from his father's identifiably Urdu-influenced English. In a more sombre example, the video left behind by the London suicide bomber Mohammad Sidique Khan, whose parents came from Pakistan but who was born in Leeds, had the unmistakeable deep tones and flat vowels of his Yorkshire upbringing.

Most speech therapists estimate that the crucial period for acquiring an accent is in early childhood, before puberty. After that, people may change the way they speak, but they will find it increasingly difficult—and they will probably never lose all traces of that first accent. Many of the parents and grandparents of today's young British Asians had learned their English in classrooms before they came to England, and for them, the outcome was very different from that of their children. Although an estimated thirty million people speak English as a matter of course in the subcontinent, the accents and intonations of indigenous Indian languages have established a range of specific and identifiable styles of speaking. Some of the difficulties are with framing the actual sounds of the language—there are no direct equivalents in Indian languages to some of the sounds used in English—but the major problem is in recreating the stress patterns of English words and sentences.

The Australian author David Malouf found himself at the sharp end of this problem after giving a lecture on literature to a learned audience in Calcutta. The president of the august literary institution which had invited him to speak thanked him, and told the audience that Mr Malouf was ready to answer questions. A bearded and bespectacled gentleman in the front row leaned forward earnestly with his hand raised. 'What do you think of this dickhead?' he asked. For a moment, Malouf was nonplussed. He glanced uneasily at the eminent and respected president of the institution, wondering briefly whether this was the particular dickhead to which the questioner was referring with such a marked lack of respect. 'I beg your pardon?' he said.

'What do you think of this dickhead? From a literary point of view?' the questioner repeated. 'How does this dickhead compare with the other dickheads we have seen?' Maybe it was divine intervention or the natural brilliance of the novelist's mind, but Malouf suddenly understood. He was being asked his opinion of the first ten years of the twenty-first century, compared with the 1990s and the 1980s which had preceded it. The questioner was interested not in the dickhead, but in the decade.

In some English words, such as *conduct* or *report*, moving the stress can make the difference between a noun and a verb—you would *conDUCT* someone to their seat, but you would complain about their *CONduct*. It's another of those rules that we obey without thinking—but it's also another of those rules that is written in sand. You could follow the example of words like *implant* or *extract*, and decide that verbs have their stress on the second syllable, and nouns on the first—but then, someone would point out *respect*. Or *exit*. Or *concern*. Or *order*. The word *protest* generally fits in with the rule, so you *proTEST*, but you make a *PROtest*—although it is one example of a word where the stress patterns seem to change according to different speakers—often leading to angry complaints to the BBC's duty log. *ReSEARCH* or *REE-search* is another. Maybe some ingenious geek could draw up a rule that took account of all the exceptions—but their ingenuity would be as nothing when compared with the subtlety with which any mother-tongue English-speaker manages to get the stresses on almost every word right every time, simply by instinct.

There are words where stress patterns differ between British and American English—*inQUIRy* against *INquiry*, for instance, or *adVERTisement* against *advertISEment*—but the fact that there are so few of them demonstrates how much agreement there is on

134

both sides of the Atlantic. We notice such words because they are exceptional—Americans, Australians, New Zealanders and South Africans, who have English as their first and often only language, almost always put the stress on the same syllable of a word as the British do. But the different stress patterns of the languages that are spoken on the subcontinent are carried over into the English spoken there, producing a version of English that can sound very different indeed.

Speakers of Malayalam, for instance, a language spoken by more than twenty-five million people in the southern Indian state of Kerala, generally give different syllables an even stress, and as a result, English teachers find their pupils frequently mispronouncing polysyllabic words. The words *police*, *dishevelled* or *whatever*, for instance, might often sound as if they are stressed on the first syllable, while *atmosphere* or *necessary* might be stressed on the second, or *celebrate*, *economic* or *hesitate* on the third. Hindi, the language spoken by about a third of the population of India, also has generally weaker stresses than English, as does Punjabi, the language of the Sikhs.

What rules English has to govern the stress in a word—for example that weak vowels are used in unstressed syllables—are followed instinctively by people who have spoken the language from birth, but present another trap to those learning it from books. Words such as *language, cricket* or *luggage,* which would all have the stress on the first syllable in most accents of English, might typically be pronounced *langWEDGE, crickETTE,* or *luggEDGE* by someone whose native language was Hindi or Malayalam, and whose natural tendency was to maintain an even stress pattern on words of more than one syllable. In fact, it's often very hard to say whether there actually is a misplaced stress or whether the lack of a distinction between stressed and unstressed syllables makes it sound as if there is. But the effect is the same.

The short unstressed *i* sound which a native English speaker might use in the final syllable of a word like *washes* or *wanted* might be replaced by a stressed *eh* sound, following the spelling. Similarly, words which have little importance to the meaning of a sentence, so-called form-words such as *and, on, the, but* or *there* in the sentence *There's bread and butter on the plate, but no jam in the dish* would normally be unstressed in English, unless the speaker was trying to achieve some special effect—but to a Hindi or Malayalam speaker, it would be natural to emphasize them in just the same way as every other word in the sentence. Some researchers in India suggest that as many as one in five of all the words in Indian English habitually has the stress placed on a different syllable from that used in the rest of the English-speaking world.

That means, of course, that native English-speakers find the same problems of stress and accent when they try to speak Indian languages. The BBC cricket commentator Christopher Martin-Jenkins was sitting with Bishen Bedi, the former Indian spin bowler, watching England play India. Throughout the day, Martin-Jenkins referred to the England player Monty Panesar—born in Luton, but the first Sikh cricketer to play for England—as *PanESSuh*, while Bedi, a Sikh like Panesar, sat beside him offering a much more correct pronunciation of the name. The stress was actually more or less even on each syllable, but to English ears, used to a falling away on the final syllable, it sounded like *PanessAR*.

For Indians speaking English, the difference in stress patterns can lead to a characteristically sing-song quality—but it can also mean they are simply not understood. Experiments show that people listening to a language being spoken pick up the meaning in several ways. First, of course, there are the sounds of vowels and consonants which make up the words—although it is easy to overemphasize the importance particularly of the vowel sounds. An interesting experiment is to replace the vowels of any sentence with a simple *uh* sound, and see how easily understood the sentence remains. *I want a plate of bacon and sausage with an egg on top—*

137

Uh wunt uh plut uv bucun und sussudge wuth un ugg un tup. You might not get what you were asking for, but it wouldn't be because you had been misunderstood.

There is also the sense of the sentence—the meaning of what is actually said. However indistinct the final consonant of the sentence *I'm going to the shop* might be, no-one would misinterpret it as *I'm going to the shot.* Few people would assume that a young man who said *I 'ate my mother-in-law* was guilty of cannibalism. But, most crucially for inexpert Indian speakers of English, there is the rhythmic pattern of the word.

The vowel-experiment with the bacon and sausage only works as long as the normal rhythms are maintained. Mistakes in comprehension made in English classes in India show how important this is. When one pupil pronounced the word *character* with the stress on the second rather than the first syllable, it was variously misheard as *director*, *erected* and *adapter*—that is, as a word with a second-syllable stress. The stress pattern had actually been more important in understanding the word than the sounds of the letters. In the same way, the word *prefer* pronounced with the stress on the first syllable was heard as *briefer*.

Confusion over particular sounds simply compounds the problems. One writer recalled his confusion in New Delhi as he listened to

Indian journalists talking animatedly about the country's 'wise president'. Surely, he thought, the world-famous independence of Indian journalism had not sunk to this level of petty sycophancy? It was only a few minutes later that he realized they were talking not about the wise president, but about the vice-president.[31] In the same way, Malayalam speakers often substitute *uh* for the *ur* sound in *turn*, to make it sound more like *tun;* there is no *zh* sound, as in the English word *measure*, and so it might be represented by an unpractised speaker of English by *ch* as in *church, z* as in *zoo*, or *s* as in *sat*, more or less indiscriminately. Hindi has no long *e* sound as in the English word *seek*, and many speakers would make no distinction between *seek* and *sick*.

None of these altered sounds would make much difference to a sentence on its own. Put together, however, along with the word- and sentence-stress patterns of Indian languages transported to English sentences, the cumulative effect of these minor changes results in a recognizable and distinct version of English, found not just across the subcontinent, but also among first-generation immigrants to the UK.

* * *

Mass immigration into Britain from the West

Indies is usually dated from the arrival of the *Windrush* in 1948—but British Black English goes back much further than people think. At the end of the eighteenth century, while learned scholars were fussing over whether it was not impossibly vulgar to say *curnel* instead of *col-o-nel*, or *fashun* for *fash-i-on*, a largely-forgotten group of English speakers was already playing its part in establishing a new version of spoken English on the streets of London. By the end of the American War of Independence in 1786, there were more than 1,200 black former slaves in London, men and women who had decided that poverty in England was preferable to slavery in the Land of the Free. The Southern States English they spoke, with its ineradicable echoes of forgotten West African languages, would have been barely comprehensible to the rest of the city.

Since then, of course, the influence of those early immigrants has been overwhelmed because of the large numbers who followed them nearly two centuries later. Those who arrived in England on the *Windrush*, and the ones who have followed, brought with them their West Indian accents, which had a similar ancestry to those of their eighteenth-century forebears. British Black English today retains some similarities with the Black English of the US, especially when it is mixed up with the language of Black American rappers—but it has developed into its own distinctive accent.

Or rather, it has developed into its own accents. The different islands and territories which make up the West Indies are scattered over more than a thousand miles of the Caribbean, and although the different native American languages which are known to have been spoken on the islands in the past are now long gone, the chopping and changing of colonial history, with British, French, Dutch and Spanish settlers arriving on the various islands at different times, means that languages and accents vary greatly from island to island. Apart from the European settlers, there have also been waves of immigration from other parts of the world, with labourers from China, West Africa and India flooding into the sugar plantations during the nineteenth century—more than a third of the population of Trinidad, for instance, is Indian, and Hindi is still commonly used among some older people of Indian descent. Then there were the dozens of mutually-incomprehensible native West African languages that arrived with the original slave population. One example that is often given of their effect on the growth of Black English is in the treatment of clusters of consonants.[32] English is rich in groups such as *st, ch* or *nd*, in which two consonants are run together, but many African languages only have a single vowel and a single consonant to each syllable. This affects the pronunciation of English, so *the* might become *te* or *de*, or *around* might be *aroun'*. All these different influences, European, Chinese, Indian and West African, have left their marks on the way that English is spoken.

That means in turn that there are differences between the accents of English spoken by people coming into Britain from the various islands. A native Barbadian, for instance, pronouncing his *r*'s in words like *farm* and *burn* like someone from the south-west of England, will sound quite different from a Trinidadian like the journalist Darcus Howe, whose *r* sounds are much more muted—*fahm* and *buhn*. Most native West Indians would be able to say with a fair degree of accuracy which island a person was from before he had spoken three sentences. But the situation in Britain is even more complex than that, because British Black English varies depending on what part of the country the speaker has settled in. In Glasgow, for instance, there may be elements of Scottish speech, or in Manchester, rounded northern *u*'s. Lenny Henry, the comedian who has made a career out of being black in much the same way as Terry Wogan has out of being Irish, makes the point. In character for one of his sketches, he can happily slip into an exaggerated West Indian accent—'Mrs Jaahnson,' he says, 'I have aalways taken a hactive hinterest in the natural werrld'—but when he speaks as himself, it is with the unmistakeable Midlands voice of Dudley, where he was born and brought up. Darcus Howe, while not claiming to be an expert on linguistics, says he can tell immediately when he meets someone in Port of Spain not only whether they have spent time in Britain, but also what part of the country they lived in.

With all these differences, it's even harder to talk about a single British Black English than it is to generalize about the various regional accents—but when most non-West Indians talk about West Indian or British Black English, they are thinking of a Jamaican accent. This is not a mark of particular approval—in fact, it is Barbados that enjoys the traditional reputation for 'good' English among the other West Indian islands, possibly because the language has been spoken there for much longer than elsewhere in the Caribbean—but rather, a result of the fact that Jamaica, with around two million people, is by far the most populous of the different islands, and is the birthplace of proportionately more black immigrants to the UK.

Even accepting the differences, there are some common factors in Black English. Long vowel sounds may be lengthened even further and picked apart, for instance, so that *Jamaican* becomes *Jumee-uh-cun*, or they may be shortened and lost altogether, so that *take* becomes *tek*. Short *a*'s and *o*'s, as in *man* and *dog*, are both generally lengthened to an *aa*-sound, giving the pronunciations *maan* and *daag*. A word like *fall* or *call*, spelled with an *a* but with an *or*-sound in most accents, would generally also be pronounced *faall* and *caall*. But where the *-or* sound is spelled as in *four* or *court*, it would be more likely to be pronounced in a double-sounding *oo-uh*, a bit like the word *brewer* in southern English. In turn, the word *show*, with an *oh* sound spelled *ow*, would make the same *oo-uh*, to give *shoo-uh*—but when spelled *o* as in *go*, the same sound in ordinary British English would be more likely to be pronounced as a short *-or*. As a result, many words that don't rhyme in standard southern English do tend to rhyme in Black English, and vice versa: *blow*, pronounced *bloo-uh*, might rhyme with *door*, pronounced *doo-uh*, but *door* would not rhyme with *jaw*, which would be pronounced *jaa*.[33] I never said it was easy to follow.

The consonants are more straightforward—but not much. *T*'s and *d*'s are often dropped at the ends of syllables when they follow *f, k* or *l*—*dohn be daf*. The *t*'s aren't usually glottalized, as they would be in Cockney or in Estuary English—when they are, it is considered to be a fairly sure sign of a native Barbadian. Among the majority of Black English speakers, they simply aren't sounded at all, so words like *ground*, *want* or *band* would be pronounced *groun*, *waan*, and *ban*. Where *d*'s and *t*'s come before an *l*, in words like *riddle* or *bottle*, they are often replaced by *g*'s and *k*'s—*riggle* and *bockle*. Initial *h*'s are often dropped, as they are in most of England, and maybe re-inserted in the wrong places, like Lenny Henry talking about his *hactive hinterest* in the natural world.

There are also different stress patterns in the language, as there are in Indian English. Whereas English words and syllables in most forms of the language are heavily stressed, Black English tends to be much more evenly and lightly stressed: the stresses in the word *animal* in standard southern English, for instance, would be *DAH-di-di*, while in Black English they would be more likely to run simply *di-di-di*, with each syllable equally stressed. At the same time, many speakers of Black English tend to pronounce more distinctly vowels which most British English speakers would reduce to a generalized *uh* sound, so that the final syllable of *animal*—just *ul* to most British English speakers—might be enunciated more clearly as *animalle*. The same thing might happen in the final syllable of words like *comma* or *government*. This, combined with the even stress pattern, can give the accent a distinctive sing-song quality in the ears of anyone not used to hearing it.

There are those who speak British Black English more broadly than others, as there are with all accents. At one extreme, it could almost be a separate language, with its own words and its own grammatical structures, while at the other, a speaker might have only the faintest trace of a Black English accent: the journalist Sir Trevor McDonald, for instance, is often quoted as an example of impeccably 'correct' pronunciation, with only a hint of his native Trinidad in the long *a*'s of words like *baad* and *attaack*, and the slightly tight *or* in *all* and *authority*. Many people, without thinking about it, would be able to choose whereabouts on that range they speak, so that children would be likely to exaggerate their accent when socializing with black friends of their own age and to tone it down considerably when talking to people who don't share the accent. It's also adopted, of course, by white teenagers and young adults who want to gain some of the street cred and cool that goes with it. It's unusual for an immigrant accent to spread outside its original boundaries in this way: the music industry, rapping and street culture have given British Black English its own status, particularly among young people. It is young people who drive the development of a language, and it will be interesting to see, over the next few decades, how much it begins to affect the wider language across the country.

But it is also important to understand another reason why young black people who were born in Britain of immigrant parents might make a positive choice to retain a West

146

Indian accent. Some don't—either consciously or unconsciously, they lose the accent of their parents as they grow up in the wider world— but many see their accent, just as Scottish or Welsh English speakers might, as a crucial part of their identity. The way you speak, as we've seen in other contexts, reveals not only who you are and where you've come from, but also who you want to be.

CHAPTER FIVE

The New Kid on the Block
American English

It's already clear from the examples of the Scots, the Welsh and the Irish that people can *speak* English without any desire at all to *be* English. Through their own accents, they can express their Scottishness, Welshness and Irishness, whatever their feelings about political union or devolution. But thanks to the British Empire, English was carried not just throughout the British Isles, but around the globe. As a result, different versions of the language have grown up as the main means of communication in North America, Australia, New Zealand, South Africa and other parts of the world. Each one has its own characteristic pronunciation, which is often more easy for a native British English speaker to recognize than it is to describe. But it is American English—the English which British traditionalists blame for unwelcome new pronunciations such as *skedule* and *soot* (for *suit*), for spellings like *color* and *aggrandize*, for oddly-tweaked little words like *persnickety*, and for grotesque monsters like *gubernatorial*, *rambunctious* or *condominium*—which raises hackles among those in Britain who see it as

148

their duty to defend the language. Politics, economics and the irresistible influence of computers and the internet mean that American English, rather than British English, is seen as the language of the twenty-first century—and that applies in Britain just as much as anywhere else.

People get angry about it, they may despise each other over it, they may get philosophical about it like George Bernard Shaw, who talked about 'two nations divided by a common language,' but no one ever quite forgets the great transatlantic squabble over how to speak. Sometimes, in our lighter moments, we sing songs about it—'You say tomayto and I say tomahto,' said George and Ira Gershwin in the 1930s, deciding it was time to call the whole thing off—but it's always there, and it always has been. The song was actually about different ways of speaking inside the United States, but it could just as well have applied to the transatlantic differences. Today, in fact, they would probably both settle for a pomodoro with a drizzle of olive oil. And in case the dispute ever gets out of proportion, it's worth remembering that they used to argue over the same red fruit in Lebanon—*banadura* or *bandura*—with less humour and more drastic results.

*   *   *

In the aftermath of the War of Independence, the Americans wanted more than a distinctive accent, like the Scots and the Irish had—they wanted a different language. It was an aggressive assertion of difference—one more example of the nationalistic use of language—and some of the greatest figures of 1776 were quite open about it. Benjamin Franklin produced a reformed alphabet and a new way of spelling for the new republic, and Thomas Jefferson, third president of the United States and author of the Declaration of Independence, predicted: 'The new circumstances under which we are placed call for new words, new phrases, and for the transfer of old words to new objects. An American dialect will therefore be formed.'[34]

Noah Webster, who sought to be as much a nation-builder with his dictionary as Jefferson was in Congress, said much the same. The separation of English and American, he declared, was necessary and unavoidable. 'Numerous local causes, such as a new country, new associations of people, new combinations of ideas in arts and sciences, and some intercourse with tribes wholly unknown in Europe, will introduce new words into the American tongue. These causes will produce in course of time a language in North America as different from the future language of England as the modern Dutch, Danish and

Swedish are from German, or from one another.'³⁵

To those causes he might have added a couple of centuries of completely different experiences, two world wars and the biggest wave of immigration the world had ever seen—but there was really no need for Franklin, Jefferson or Webster to trouble themselves. Webster's dictionary did as much as a book could to establish American English in its own right, but that would have happened eventually whether he had picked up his pen or not. The Americans of the later eighteenth century should have known better than anyone that language, especially spoken language, is the ultimate democracy. It was just as futile for Webster to complain as he did about the 'affectation' of a particular, supposedly English, way of rounding the letter *a* into *ah* in words like *grass* as it was more than 200 years later for parents in England to grumble over their children's Americanisms. You can't tell people how to speak.

In fact, the gulf between the English spoken on the two sides of the Atlantic owed at least as much to the conservatism of the settlers as it did to any effort to establish differences between the two nations. Franklin, in the late eighteenth century, was still insisting on the pronunciation of the *l* in words such as *would* and *should*, long after it had been abandoned by English speakers in

151

Britain. Webster similarly insisted on the 'correct' pronunciation of *deaf* as *deef*, hanging on to a vowel sound that had been abandoned in most of Britain. (It is only the Scots who have retained it on the British side of the Atlantic, giving rise to a piece of rhyming slang that the English find completely incomprehensible. 'Do ye think Ah'm corned beef?')

Occasionally, this tendency to cling to original pronunciations had a slightly twisted history, as it did with the *oi*-sound in words like *boil*, *poison* or *join*. Around the time of the first settlements, the sound had been pronounced in Britain like the *eye* sound of words like *wine*, as we've seen in looking at the development of the Irish accent. That *eye* sound is the pronunciation that travelled to America, and the words remained much the same on that side of the Atlantic at least until the mid-eighteenth century. Slang speech maintained the habit for a long time after that, so pronunciations such as *jine*, *bile* and *pisen* were common. The word *roil*, descended from a French word meaning to stir up, was commonly used in the eighteenth century to mean *infuriate* or *anger*. It has virtually vanished from the language—but the word *rile*, now spelled to match its pronunciation, survives. The original pronunciation, lost in most of Britain, but preserved in American slang, has created a new word of its own. The short vowels of seventeenth-century England, in words like *creature* and *sleek*, also survived much longer in America, giving pronunciations of *critter* and *slick*. In the latter case, in fact, another new word has been created, this time alongside the old. President Bill Clinton might have been more flattered to be referred to as 'sleek Willy' rather than 'slick Willy'. Similarly, Americans clung to the short vowel in the word *saucy*—and now the word *sassy* has achieved a life of its own on both sides of the Atlantic.

There are occasional stories of a community somewhere in New England or Virginia, depending on who is telling them, who speak almost exactly as the original settlers of the late seventeenth and early eighteenth centuries did—stories, in fact, that the language of Shakespeare, a bit like Elvis or Buddy Holly, is alive and well and living on the East Coast of the United States. Leaving aside the fact that no one knows exactly what the language of Shakespeare sounded like, and the inconvenient failure of anyone to produce these bizarre cultural throwbacks and invite them on to television or into a recording studio, the stories ignore one crucial reality: nothing escapes evolution.

Even professional linguists occasionally fall into the trap of assuming that so-called indigenous languages can somehow survive down the centuries unchanged, but as long as

153

they are living languages, learned and used by people in their daily lives rather than studied from books like Latin or Sanskrit, they all change and develop. The Welsh, Cornish, Breton and Basque of the twentieth century, where they survive, are different from the languages of the seventeenth, and in the same way, the English spoken by the settlers in America three centuries ago has gone through changes from generation to generation. There is no 'Lost Plateau' where the speech of the past can still be heard.

But the story of the lost Elizabethans holds a kernel of truth: the settlers did bring the language of the seventeenth century with them, and odd, random bits of it survive in the grammar and accents of the Americans of today. Pronouncing *roil* as *rile* was one of them—but there were others. Britain was for many years a larger, more cosmopolitan society than that of America, and there were more outside influences on the way the language was spoken. It is a commonplace in the study of the history of languages to note that a small and isolated community, like that of the early American settlers, will tend to cling to old ways of speaking much more tenaciously than one which is expanding and changing.

That's what happened. The so-called 'Continental *i*', which makes *oblige* sound like *obleege*, was correct in the England that the settlers left behind them, and survived in America long after it had become obsolete in England. That has gone, but other words simply appeared, apparently of their own volition: the last letter of the alphabet, referred to so disrespectfully by Shakespeare in *King Lear* when Kent calls Oswald 'Thou whoreson zed! Thou unnecessary letter!' became *zee* in America during the eighteenth century and remains so today. The new word was apparently created by analogy with the other consonants, *b*, *c*, *d*, and so on, although *zee* was occasionally used as an alternative form in England as far back as 1677. *Webster's Dictionary* in 1828 settled the matter for America by declaring, 'Z . . . is pronounced *zee.*' Even so, the US remains the only place where *zee* is generally used, although it is spreading with television, films and the internet.

What survived of all these original pronunciations, what was lost, and what was invented was largely a matter of chance: the point is that British English and American English started from the same place back in the early eighteenth century, and developed independently of each other. A hundred years ago, when New England was ruled by the aristocratic Boston Brahmins, wealthy colonial families like the Lowells and the Cabots, the otherwise unknown John Collins Bossidy raised a glass at a dinner at Holy Cross

College. His toast became the famous description of Boston's agriculture, its fisheries, and its social exclusivity:

So this is good old Boston,
The home of the Bean and the Cod,
Where Lowells talk only to Cabots,
And the Cabots talk only to God.

Many New Englanders believed that the rounded *a*'s and dropped *r*'s of the upper-crust Boston accent were correct, traditional pronunciations. Bossidy's audience would have been thoroughly convinced that they, as well as the Lowells, the Cabots, and probably God himself, spoke in the accents of the Protestant English settlers who had originally founded the city. Certainly the old catchphrase 'Park the car in Harvard Yard' still sounds perfectly natural to a modern British ear when a Bostonian strips it of the *r* sounds that other American accents might put into it—*pahk the cah in Hahvid Yahd*, rather than *parrk the carr in Harrv'd Yarrd*—and the familiar *aw* of *Bawst'n* was found in several English dialects around the sixteenth and seventeenth centuries. But the diners at Holy Cross were mistaken. Noah Webster, writing in 1789, shows that the rounded New England *a*, which is so similar to the *a* of southern England, and which led one native Bostonian to observe, 'My mom's sister is my ahnt—ants crawl on the ground. Well, maybe your ahnt does that too . . .' was an imitation of a contemporary eighteenth-century English fashion, not a well-preserved piece of settler-English. Webster makes words like *wrath*, *bath* and *path* rhyme with *hath*, as they do in most American accents, and complains bitterly about the 'affectation' of self-consciously English pronunciations that round the *a* to make the words rhyme with *garth*, as the Bostonians did and do. Even *aunt* is given a flat *a* in Webster's list—and in fact, most linguistic historians say that there was no *ah* sound in English until the late-eighteenth century, when fashionable London people began to copy it from the French, and Bostonians began to copy it from them.

By that account at least, then, the Boston Brahmins were not so much the inheritors of the pure accents of their hard-working pioneer ancestors as the offspring of a foppish clique of eighteenth-century socialites. Language often plays such tricks—there are no straight lines in its development, and claims of linguistic purity generally turn out to be embarrassingly bogus. When Bossidy was raising his glass, in fact, the exclusivity of the Protestant Brahmin caste and certainly that of their supposedly pure accent were under sustained attack from waves of Irish and Italian immigrants, who flooded into Boston in the second half of the nineteenth-century.

Holy Cross itself, where Bossidy made his speech, was a Jesuit foundation. Evolution doesn't stop, even for the Lowells and the Cabots.

The Bostonians' *r* sound, too, reflects a fashion that grew up a hundred years or more after their settler ancestors arrived in America. In fact, the rhotic *r* divides the US just as much as it divides the west of England from the rest of the country, or Scotland from England. Across most of the US apart from New England, *r* is pronounced wherever it appears in a word, so most Americans would talk about a *ladderr* or a *carrpet* just as Englishmen in the seventeenth century would have done. So, to this day, as we've seen, do people in the west of England, in Scotland and Ireland. But in England, around the start of the eighteenth century, people started to drop the *r* sound, so they would have said *ladduh* or *cahpet*, as they do in modern British English. That habit— non-rhotic speech—travelled to Australia, New Zealand and South Africa with the settlers of the eighteenth and nineteenth centuries.

The Anglophile Henry James, returning to the US in 1905 with his reputation as a novelist at its height after twenty-five years in Europe, declared witheringly that the audible American *r*—the sound which the Cabots and Lowells despised, the pronunciation of most of the rest of America—sounded to him like 'a sort of morose grinding of the back teeth'.**36** Well, maybe—but James, the Lowells, the Cabots and the rest of the Boston Brahmin elite were wrong if they saw their own speech as reflecting the accents of the original American settlers. It is the rest of America, morose or not, that is closer to the pronunciation of seventeenth-century England.

Elizabethan Englishmen, too, would have been more likely to pronounce the *oo* vowel of *duty*, *duke* or *new* in the same way as many Americans would today—without the *y*-sound before the *oo* which causes so much angst to British English speakers. H. L. Mencken, writing in 1921, produced a complex rule to describe the usual US practice in dealing with words like *dyuty*, *dyuke* or *nyew*, which developed their *yoo* in England during the eighteenth century. Americans, he said, 'retain it following *m*, *f*, *v* and *p*, and usually before *r*, but they are careless about it following *n* and *g*, and drop it following *l*, *r*, *d*, *t*, *th* and *s*.' It is as accurate as most rules about language—people on both sides of the Atlantic would say *myule* or *pyuny*, and many Americans would certainly say *dooty*, *toon* or *loot* (for *lute*)—but however closely they obey the rule, not one person in a million could spell it out. And of course in the word *figure*, where the most fastidious British English speaker would say *figger*, many Americans would say *figyure*. Go figure, as they say.

Henry James could get over-excited—on another occasion, he referred to late nineteenth-century spoken English in America as 'the confused, the ugly, the flat, the thin, the mean, the helpless, that reduce articulation to an ignoble minimum . . . a mere helpless slobber of disconnected vowel noises.'[37] But his contempt for the language of his own native land points up one constant theme that has run through the pronunciation of English in the US ever since the days of Noah Webster. On one side, fired with patriotic fervour and a dislike of 'affectation', were those who distrusted people they called 'Anglomaniacs', whom they accused of aping every new London fashion, while on the other—mainly on the eastern seaboard, where transatlantic contact was easier—were people who found an insistence on General American and its difference from Britain unsophisticated and provincial. James's exaggerated distaste for the American *r* sound shows how irrational this prejudice could be—but it's a mirror image of the grumbling in Britain about 'Americanisms', which continually shifts its ground as different expressions and pronunciations cease to grate on native ears and become accepted. In the Britain of the mid-twentieth century, for instance, the word *nephew* was pronounced with the *v* sound of its French root, even though it had been spelled with a *ph* for more

160

than 300 years. The American pronunciation with a softer *f* was first anachronistic, then annoying, and finally accepted. Much the same has happened with words like *diphthong* and *diphtheria*, where the Americans' refusal to try to twist their tongues round the awkward *f-th* sound has been widely adopted in Britain—although it seems odd that people should find that combination of sounds so difficult when they can manage phrases like *half the time* without any trouble. It's presumably simply the spelling that makes *diptheria*, not *dipp-theria*, seem like the more attractive option. Whatever the reason is, once the new pronunciation has been accepted, few people in Britain would even notice the difference. In the same way, the American *r* would have sounded new, strange, and hopelessly provincial to Henry James after his long stay in London.

But the argument, of course, has always been about more than just the sound of words. In 1832, Mrs Frances Trollope, the mother of the novelist, observed tartly that in her travels around America, she had very seldom heard 'a sentence elegantly turned and correctly pronounced from the lips of an American. There is always something either in the expression or the accent that jars the feelings and shocks the taste.'**38** How grandly she refers to 'the feelings' and 'the taste' when she means 'my feelings' and 'my taste'—and with

161

what enviable assurance she assumes that she can decide the elegance of a sentence or the correctness of an accent. What she is criticizing here is a whole culture and a whole way of life, rather than a simple style of speech. The shocking accent, she declared, was largely due to the thin and compressed lips of American men, caused by the need to prevent the tobacco they chewed from slipping out—a diagnosis which ignores American women and men who don't chew tobacco, but which no doubt drew superior smiles from her audience at home.

And of course, the Americans could give at least as good as they got. A few decades after Mrs Trollope, Sylvia Clapin produced a *Dictionary of Americanisms*. She had nothing to learn from the other side of the Atlantic, she said. 'As a matter of fact, and as regards the great bulk of the people of the United States, there can be no question but that they speak purer and more idiomatic English than do the masses in the Old Country.' Leave out the point that, as a matter of fact, her sentence is a matter of opinion, and forget that, even if we accept her analysis, then 'purer English' simply means 'more old-fashioned English'— Mrs Clapin, like Mrs Trollope before her, is mounting a wider attack than she admits.

Nearly a hundred years on, and Emily Post was making much the same disguised nationalistic point, although this time she was concentrating on her own city of New York. The New York accent, she said, was—well—non-existent. 'On the whole, New York has no accent since it is a composite of all in one,' she declared, unintentionally giving a perfect example of the common belief, held in London just as fervently as in New York, that one's own metropolitan accent is the unalloyed gold-standard of pronunciation.

'To a New York ear, which ought to be fairly unbiased since the New York accent is a composite of all accents, English women chirrup and twitter,' she said. Her more important points, though, were aimed not at bird-like English women, but at socially ambitious New Yorkers. 'Such differences as between saying *wash* or *wawsh*, *adVERTisement* or *advertISEment* are of small importance. But no one who makes the least pretence of being a person of education says *kep* for *keep*, *genulmun* or *gempmun*, or *lay-dee*, *vawde-vil* or *eye-talian*.'

Why one group of differences matters more than the other, she doesn't say—people like her seldom do. But all these writers are waving their language in the air the same way that a demagogue might wave a flag. They are saying that their own speech, their own way of life, is at the centre of the world. Whether it is a 'fairly unbiased' New Yorker or an English *grande dame* with 'feelings' and 'taste', anything that is unfamiliar is bizarre, vulgar, or degenerate. By criticizing the way that other people speak, they are implicitly declaring their own superiority.

Mrs Post at least had no doubt—but there has often been a considerable degree of confusion on both sides of the Atlantic about what is desirable. Even the Gershwins' distinction between *tomahto* and *tomayto* has not always been universally accepted. The gloriously-named English watercolourist, Evacustes A. Phipson, complained bitterly in the early 1920s: 'It is really distressing to a cultivated Briton visiting America to find people there who . . . follow what they suppose to be the latest London mannerism, regardless of accuracy. Thus we find one literary editress advocating the pedantic British pronunciation *tomahto* in lieu of the good English *tomato*, rhyming with *potato*, saying it sounds so much more refined . . . Similarly, we sometimes hear Anglomaniac Americans saying *vahz* for *vase*. Why not also *bahz* and *cahz*?'**39** (The words he was referring to, of course, were *base* and *case*, not *bars* and *cars*.) Phipson certainly saw himself as defending 'correct' pronunciation, but he was being, according to your pronunciation, either pernickety or persnickety, since the rounded *a* in *vase* dated back at least to the eighteenth century in British English. It remains *vahs* in Britain, although *vawz* used to be heard. In America, people say *vaiz, vace, vahz, vahce, vawz* and *vawce*. Families have been known almost to come to blows over it.

The cultivated Mr Phipson may have been less distressed to find that Americans, then and now, often seem to speak their words with more care than the most pedantic speaker of British English—*secretary* or *extraordinary*, for instance, would normally be pronounced *secr't'ry* and *extr'ord'n'ry* in Britain, while an American speaker would sound each syllable. But it would be foolish to be too dogmatic about the superiority of American pronunciation: the *-ile* part of words like *missile* or *fertile* is choked off as a final *'l* in American English. Ogden Nash makes the point, in his poem about the turtle, where he rhymes *turtle* and *fertile*. And the Southern States *prah'l'm*, or *problem*, is only one of many words where the stretched-out US vowel sound has entirely swallowed the word's consonant.

The American humorist and cartoonist James Thurber grumbled that when he was growing up in the mid-West, it often seemed that the inoffensive little letter *o* seemed to be about to drop out of the language. He had no problem with *possum* taking over from *opossum*, he said, but he noted tetchily that *official* often came out as *fishel*, and *obituary* as *bituary*. Unstressed syllables like those initial *o*'s are often vulnerable—but once you've noticed a particular change in the language, it can start to grate. That's what Thurber found, anyway.

But in any case, if America's vowels have been in general carefully protected, the consonants have suffered an attack that has in some cases almost wiped them out. *Prah'l'm* is one much-mimicked example from the Southern States, but the emasculation of the middle *t* in words like *letter, butter* or *writer* is widespread across the whole US. Most British English speakers would pronounce a central *t* with the tongue slightly higher in the mouth than it would be for one which came at the beginning of a word, but that tendency is carried to much greater lengths in American English, so that, as we saw in an earlier chapter, *writer* and *rider*, or *latter* and *ladder* sound almost exactly the same. A word like *tighter* makes the point, with an initial *tuh* followed by a *d*-sound in the middle. On the other hand, if the British should start to feel smug about the way they have defended their *t*'s, they might reflect that the rampant glottal stop of so-called Estuary English, which turns *bottle* into *bo'ull* and *letter* into *le'uh* is almost unknown in North America. In fact, when an American wants to destroy a consonant, he does it completely. The *t*'s in *latter* and *writer* are changed to a liquid *d*-sound, but where there is an *n* before a *t*, such as in the words *winter* or *banter*, the sound virtually vanishes, to make them sound the same as *winner* or

166

banner.

Initial *h*'s, though, are practically a protected species in the US when compared with Britain. Turning *hat* into *'at*, as many British speakers do, has never been an American *'abit*—although here again, French influence made itself felt in the loss of *h*'s from words such as *herb*—where the English keep the *h*—or *hotel*—where they can't make their minds up. It's also noticeable that the Americans took the French *Nouveau Orleans*, battered the words into submission, and turned them completely into English, with an all-American *N'Aw* to begin with, an *ee* sound in the middle to replace the nasalized *ay-on* of the French, and the silent French final *s* defiantly brought back to life *N'Awleens*. The British *Nyew Orlee-uns*, by contrast, goes only halfway, pronouncing the final *s*, but giving the central vowel a peculiar *ee-uh* sound that is presumably meant to echo the original French. But then, the British, as we will see in a later chapter, have a love-hate relationship with French words. They hate the way we pronounce them, and we love it.

Despite Emily Post and her friends, America has never had anything like the class-consciousness associated with language that has plagued Britain—but even in the world's first great immigration melting-pot, foreign pronunciations have always been stigmatized. The influx of European Jews, especially into

New York, brought people whose first language was Yiddish, and who were uncomfortable with the *er* sound of *bird* and *pearl*. The British journalist C. V. R. Thompson, travelling to the US in the 1930s to take up a job for the *Daily Express*, found himself lost at first without the familiar class distinctions of British English pronunciation, but soon homed in on the sounds of urban New York. 'Of course, I realized that someone who calls a pearl a *poil* or an oyster an *ester* does not quite belong. And I could recognise the *dese*, *dem* and *dose* guys as definitely lower stratum.'[40]

D's for *th*'s, like *poils* and *boids*, were also a European Jewish change, although other groups such as Black Americans in the south and Germans in the north-east, did much the same thing. All Thompson was really doing was spotting immigrant pronunciations. Spanish settlers also brought their language with them, most obviously in place names like Rio Grande or Los Angeles. Just as Jewish immigrants had trouble with *th*'s and *er*'s, so the Spanish-speaking settlers confused *sh* and *ch*, so that *church* might be pronounced *shurch*, *chursh* or even *shursh*. In return, non-Spanish-speakers, trying to reproduce Spanish words in English, produced their own manglings, so that the Spanish verb *saber*, to know, became *savvy*. (The letter *b* often changes to a *v*—just try saying a *b* sound

168

without closing your lips completely, and you will see why.) Similarly, East Coast sophisticates in the nineteenth century trying to describe a particular way of walking by using the French dancing term *chassée*, came up with *sashay*. Formal French dancing masters of the day might be horrified to find the term applied to the sexy, self-confident swagger of a model on a cat-walk, but the pronunciation, and then the word, have acquired lives of their own.

But although, as Thompson noticed, some sounds became associated with immigrant communities, he couldn't make the same assumptions as he did in England. At home in London, the rule was strict: the broader a man's local accent, the lower down the social scale he would be assumed to belong. Education and peer pressure would squeeze the geographical identity out of his speech. The simplest test in London, the dropped *h* as in *I 'aven't 'ad an 'am sandwich*, was completely missing. 'There was no Cockney accent in New York, and everyone pronounced a perfect *h*,' Thompson observed, with some perplexity, as he continued to try to decipher what seemed to him to be a complete social jumble. 'Those who were very carefree with *doesn't*, *asked* and *kept*, pronouncing them so that their mouth looked like a doughnut walking upstairs, were usually the ones who did not belong.' That was a rough rule of

169

thumb for New York, but it was hard to find a rule that would separate rich from poor that would apply across the States: more generally it was true to say that an upper-class Bostonian would sound very different from an upper-class Texan.

But even there, there was no certainty to be found for the sadly-perplexed Thompson. If he had travelled far outside his New York base, he might have been just as confused over the lack of local accents. For all the differences between the Deep South and the Yankee north, between New England and California, the English of the US was, and is, much less fragmented than that spoken in Britain. At home, Thompson or anyone else might have had a fair stab at identifying a native of Liverpool, Birmingham, Leeds or Plymouth by the way he spoke, but in the US, most people Thompson would have met would have spoken General American—a range of broadly similar accents that are not immediately identifiable as coming from a particular part of the country. The fact that an expert like Henry Lee Smith should demonstrate his ability to deduce where people came from by their accent on a radio programme shows how difficult it could be. And no one else has rivalled his skill since the 1940s. In areas where people have been speaking English for many centuries—the different regions of England, for example, or in Wales—there has been time

170

for different accents to grow up and establish themselves. In the US, the same is true to a lesser degree in the Southern States and on the East Coast, but elsewhere, where settlements have been more recent, there are fewer differences in the way people speak. It's the same in other parts of the world where English settlers arrived in numbers within the last two to three hundred years: people may have Australian, New Zealand or South African accents, but wherever they live in those countries, their speech will be more or less the same.

There was another strand to the history of American speech: immigration was not always a matter of choice. Slave traders reported that the human cargo they brought to America in the seventeenth, eighteenth and nineteenth centuries spoke a huge variety of mutually incomprehensible languages, but the West African language Wolof established itself for some time as a common tongue among many slaves in the Southern States. It also brought a few words of its own into the language, often through the medium of black music—the Wolof *hipi* means to see or be aware, and survives in English as *hip*, while the slang *dig*, meaning to like or sympathize with, comes from the Wolof *degg*, to understand.

Influenced by the English of the slave-owners, and by the other African languages of the slave population, Wolof developed into

171

several pidgin dialects and creoles such as Sranan, in the British slave colony of Surinam on the northern coast of South America, and Gullah, which is still common on the Sea Islands off the coast of Georgia and South Carolina. The vocabularies of these simple languages were overwhelmingly based on English, but the grammar and much of the pronunciation came from Wolof and other African languages. The Gullah version of the Lord's Prayer makes the point:

> Ow-uh farruh, hu aht in heh-wm, hallow-ed be dy name, dy kingdom come, dy will be done on ut as it done in heh-wn. Jih-w us dis day ow-uh daylih bread, an fejih-w dohz truspuss ajens us. Lead us not into temptation, but dihlih-wuh us fum all ting like e-wull. Dyne dih kingdom, pahwuh, an dy glorih.[41]

The *w*'s for *v*'s, the *d*'s for *th*'s, and the *-uh* replacing final *r*-sounds all carried over into Southern States black American pronunciation of English. That, certainly, was what Joel Chandler thought in the 1880s, when he published his *Bre'r Rabbit* stories, and put them in the mouth of Uncle Remus. Another feature of Gullah, carried over from its West African roots, is that it has no words with initial unstressed syllables, so that such English words as *respect*, *obtain* or *allow* are often pronounced *'spect*, *'tain* and *'low*.

All these influences, slight in themselves, combined to take the spoken English of America further away from the language of Britain, which was developing all the time in its own different directions. As C. V. R. Thompson found to his confusion, there has never been the same linkage in the United States between accent and social class that the British have become used to, but the growth of General American has provided a standard form of the language which foreign speakers aim to copy. Many Americans would think of it as 'accentless' in much the same way as British speakers would think of RP or BBC English.

A few features can be identified in it—the rhotic *r* in words such as *pearl*, *car* and *court*, and the merger of the vowel sounds in *father* and *brother*. The liquid *d*-sound in words such as *matter* is another common element, so that words such as *matter* and *madder*, *grater* and *grader*, or *metal* and *medal* sound the same or almost the same. Breaking a language down into its basic sound-systems always seems to diminish it—but put together, those changes add up to the difference between Tony Blair and George Bush, between John Wayne and Hugh Grant.

*   *   *

But there's another lesson to be learned in

Britain from the way English is spoken—and heard—in the US. Since we hardly ever appreciate how we speak ourselves, it's useful to hear how other people *think* we speak. Americans, for instance, often mimic the *r* sound in British English as a *d*, so that *very* becomes *veddy*. When Americans want to make fun of a British accent, that's one feature they pick on: an article in the *Detroit News*, for instance, described Rolls-Royce as 'a veddy British approach to automobiles.'[42]

It's become a cliché whenever American journalists want to paint a picture of the 'traditional' England of fallen-down castles, warm beer, Toby jugs and Received Pronunciation. A *Washington Post* headline describing two new pubs that had opened in the city with features like an Oxford rowing shell hanging from the ceiling, an imitation log fire burning in a stone fireplace, and a royal coat of arms above the door, ran 'Veddy Good—two English pubs join the crowd'.[43] A British English speaker might be nonplussed—after all, he might argue, *veddy* is what Indian speakers of English say: *veddy, veddy good*.

And that is the clue to what is happening. American speakers tend to pronounce their *r*'s more strongly than most speakers of British English. A weaker *r*, sounded as it is with a slight tap of the tongue on the alveolar ridge behind the front teeth, can sound to someone who pronounces the sound a little further back

174

in the mouth, as Americans do, like a slightly thick *d*—and so, with the instinctive exaggeration that comes when somebody wants to make a point, *veddy* becomes the American interpretation of the English pronunciation of the word. Many Indian speakers of English, in turn, will pronounce the sound even further forward in their mouths—which, to British English speakers, has the same effect of making the *r* sound almost like a thickened *d*.

Some English speakers, of course, make much more of a *d*-like sound when they pronounce their *r*'s than others—Scouse is an obvious example—while others, like Bristolians and people from the south-west, sound their *r*'s as clearly as any American. But that's not part of the American *perception* of British English: just as the new pubs in Washington represent England as a land of Oxford rowing eights, stone arches, Big Ben, and black London taxis, so *veddy, veddy good* has become England's image in the States. What we hear is often what we imagine we hear.

*   *   *

When the question is asked, 'Why do the British and the Americans speak so differently?' it might be helpful to frame it slightly differently. If instead, we ask: 'Isn't it odd that two peoples living 4,000 miles apart for 200 years, with little direct verbal communication for more than half that time, should speak differently?' it becomes easier to find the answer, 'No, not very.'

In fact, although the age of instant communication has brought the languages closer together in some ways, there are still times when different words, different grammatical habits, and different pronunciations can leave an American at Heathrow or a British traveller at JFK completely bewildered. It is still commented on if an actor from one side of the Atlantic manages to cultivate a successful accent from the other, like the British actor Hugh Laurie, who even managed a scene as an American doctor speaking with a bad British accent in the television series *House*, or the American Renée Zellweger in *Bridget Jones*. The British television producer who was congratulated by a New York taxi-driver on 'How well you speak our language' was probably just unlucky or, more likely, simply being teased—but there is no doubt that there is a gulf between Britain and America in our day-to-day speech, and that it is probably getting bigger. Recent research by computer scientists at Brunel University suggests that British speakers have a steeper rise and fall in the pitch of their voices, and that they shorten their vowels compared with Americans—changes which can confuse the voice recognition software on computers to increase error rates by more than 100 per cent. It's always good to hear about computers being fooled.

For the future, it seems fairly clear that Hugh Laurie's talent—adopting an American accent—may become the more valuable accomplishment. Just as economic and commercial power spread English around the world from the sixteenth century on, first to North America and then to Australia, New Zealand, Africa and India, so economic and commercial power in the twenty-first century is already resulting in the growth of American English. And yet there is one reason to suppose that British English may yet have some fight left in it. Just as the British have always found a French accent to be irredeemably sexy, so the Americans allegedly come all over goose-bumps at the sound of a non-rhotic *r* and a rounded *a*. Tony Blair's 22-year-old son Euan, off to work for a few months at the US Congress in Washington, was promised by a fellow-Brit who wrote in the newspapers about his own year there, 'A British accent is great for pulling power. Euan is onto a winner here. The girls even loved my posh pinstripes.' Young men boasting about how sexually attractive they are may not always be the most reliable witnesses, but the suggestion does offer an insight into one possible future for British English. After all,

Britain already has a reputation for a dusty and slightly retro sort of stylishness; and the Americans don't play soccer in any great numbers. So while the trade, business and diplomacy of the twenty-first century may be carried out in button-down-collared General American, elocutionists in London may still hope to make themselves a living polishing the RP accents of the next generation of butlers, footballers and gigolos.

CHAPTER SIX

Convicts, Colonists and the
All-important Butterfly
Australia, New Zealand and South Africa

Sir Walter Raleigh's cousin, Sir Richard Grenville—the same one who, six years later, was to captain the *Revenge* in its last ill-fated battle with the Spanish—landed on Roanoke Island towards the end of the sixteenth century to establish the first English settlement in the new world of the Americas. When he came ashore, he was starting a process that would lead to the spread of the English language all over the world. It didn't seem like it at the time—the settlement on the coast of what was eventually to become the United States was deserted again within a year—but the English spoken there has developed and evolved over four centuries into the closest thing the world has ever had to a truly global language.

It is the first language for more than 300 million people and a second language for hundreds of millions more. During the two centuries that followed the establishment of the settlement in Virginia, the growing British Empire took English to Australia, New Zealand, Canada, Nigeria, Kenya, South Africa, India, the West Indies and the Far

East. In some of these places, the empire-builders found large numbers of native peoples speaking their own languages, which had a marked effect on the pronunciation and development of the English that was spoken there. In India, as we have seen, the sounds of Hindi, Bengali, Gujarati and the other Indo-Aryan languages of south Asia are all echoed in the way English is spoken today, while in Africa, Gikuyu, Yoruba, Xhosa, Ibo, Zulu and the Afrikaans of the Dutch settlers of South Africa have all similarly left their mark. Languages change each other, like different paints poured into a pot.

In the Americas, and then in Australia and New Zealand, the English-speaking settlers also found native people with their own languages—but in these places, the local inhabitants were rapidly conquered, economically exploited, and in many cases largely wiped out by European diseases and the hunger for land. There is an occasional echo of their languages in the way English is spoken, particularly in the case of place-names, but the overall influence has been slight. Their descendants today may speak their own variety of English, but the overwhelming majority of English speakers are descendants either of the original settlers or of later immigrants. Some of the words they have assimilated from the indigenous languages have been accepted into the wider language—

hurricane, for instance, comes originally from the West Indian Taino word *huracan*, and *kangaroo* and *kookaburra* are derived from one of the Australian aborigine languages—but for the most part, the language has developed independently.

As we saw in America, small, self-contained communities like the settlements which the original settlers founded in Australia and New Zealand tend to be more conservative in their speech than the expanding and cosmopolitan countries of Europe from which they came. Apart from the limited effect of indigenous languages, there are fewer outside influences to change them, and so they hold on longer to the pronunciations and habits of speech which were common when they were founded. But there have been differences in their history which have led to the development of the different accents which we know today.

An Australian nanny is said to have visited a bookstore in downtown New York, and asked earnestly for books on dog disease. The assistant, slightly puzzled, led her to the rather restricted section of the shop dealing with pet care, and offered to try to find a book with a section on the illnesses that can affect dogs. The nanny, even more puzzled, explained: 'No, no, Dog-Disease. He writes for children— you know, the *Cat and the Hat* and *How the Grinch Stole Christmas . . .*' Not many people would relish being known as Dog-Disease—

but Dr Seuss, whose famous children's book, *Green Eggs and Ham*, used only fifty different words from start to finish, might at least have been amused by the way the sound of words changes.

*   *   *

Languages, by their very nature, don't have birthdays. Except for made-up ones like Esperanto—and how many people grow up speaking Esperanto?—they aren't created, they grow, imperceptibly, over generations and centuries. The people who speak them find they need new ways of expressing themselves, gradually shifting the way they pronounce vowels and consonants, inventing their own words and borrowing others from various sources. It is impossible to draw a firm boundary between an accent and a dialect, or between a dialect and a language, and so there is never a date on which you can say a language begins.

Except for Strine.

Strine was born in 1965, when a Scottish designer called Alistair Morrison took the pseudonym Afferbeck Lauder and wrote *Let Stalk Strine*. The foreword was written by Freud I. Breakface, and the illustrations provided by Al Terego—the jokes are quite clear when you get into the swing of Strine. The book drew on a tradition of self-mocking

Australian humour, which led to characters like Edna Everage and Sir Les Patterson, and it gave birth to a new language. It can be hard for an outsider to interpret—try phrases like *Spin-Ear Mitch*, which means 'exact replica' as in 'He's the Spin-Ear Mitch of his old man', or 'Soym gwynn, butter dinsim caimairt,' which translates as 'I saw him go in, but I didn't see him come out'. *Strine* itself, of course, is a sort of run-together version of *Australian*; *Affabeck Lauder* is *Alphabetical Order* and *Freud I. Breakface* is *Friday Breakfast*. It can get addictive: how might a well-bred English lady respond to a social invitation like *whine cher comoveren avtee?* Or how long would it take to get to the hairdresser's after being told *yuma sketcher rare cut?*

The story is that Morrison was inspired to write his book after reading an account in the *Sydney Morning Herald* of a book-signing, in which the English novelist Monica Dickens solemnly inscribed one of her books 'To Emma Chisit, from Monica Dickens'—before realizing, too late, that the purchaser had not been giving her name, but simply asking her how much it cost. It doesn't take much of a sense of humour to see that the joke was really on the buttoned-up English rather than the Australians, which is presumably one reason why Morrison's book—or rather, Afferbeck Lauder's book—was so well-received in Australia.

It came, too, at just the right moment in Australia's history, when the country was starting to fight back against more than a hundred years of disparaging criticism of its distinctive way of speaking. The attacks had not always come from outside—in fact, the English traveller James Dixon wrote in 1822 that 'the children born in those colonies, and now grown up, speak a better language, purer, more harmonious than is generally the case in most parts of England'[44]—but what the New South Wales School Commission described thirty years later as the 'vicious pronunciation' of young Australians in its care became a standard complaint in newspapers and public statements. There were suggestions, usually made by Australians themselves, that their 'slow, drawling speech' was a mark of mental and physical laziness, and that people in the southern hemisphere simply failed to open their mouths properly when they spoke. An imaginative array of medical diagnoses was offered for what was called the 'colonial twang'—in 1901, a doctor declared there was a 'national predisposition to naso-pharyngeal disease', while another suggested in 1943 that pollen in the air causing a national 'inflammation of the nose' was having the same effect.[45] Others, looking to their history rather than their noses, blamed the convicts for bringing their Cockney accents with them on the prison ships. The *Sydney Bulletin* in

January 1894, for instance, wrote in terms that might have earned an Englishman a punch on the nose. 'Ghastly nonsense is lavished upon the subject of "colonial twang",' the paper wrote in a lengthy editorial. 'The early English convicts, mostly from London, brought it with them. Early Australian parents were too busy, and generally too uneducated, to notice that their offspring had caught the complaint, and said *kike* for *cake* and *gripes* for *grapes* . . .'

An Australian judge at the Sydney Quarter Sessions in November 1933 had a little lawyerly fun at the expense of the language: 'It is a maxim recognized wherever the English language is spoken and in some places where it is not, including the University of Sydney, that you cannot convict a man on suspicion,' he said, presumably in tones not unlike those of the British judge a few years later who asked who The Beatles were. And then there was Jock Marshall, an Australian hero of World War II and a scientist at Sydney University with an impeccable New South Wales pedigree, who wrote about the Australian accent in 1942: 'Of all the accents evolved by British-speaking man, it is . . . by far the most unpleasant.'[46]

It's hardly surprising, after all this breast-beating and self-criticism, that Afferbeck Lauder's ironic who-cares-anyway shrug of the shoulders should have been a welcome change. 'The Australians are not, after all, an English-

185

speaking people . . . they only think they speak English, but in reality speak Strine,' Morrison observed.[47] But having defined Strine and given lists of examples of the language for readers to pick over, he said nothing about where it had come from or how it had developed.

Certainly, as the *Sydney Bulletin* noted with its references to *cake* and *kike*, or *grapes* and *gripes*, there were aspects of the Australian accent that echo the London English of the nineteenth century. There still are. The *o* sound in *hope* is generally pronounced as *ow*, while the *ow* diphthong in *cow* (*a-oo*) is lengthened to a triphthong *eeow*. (A *diphthong* is two sounds run together: if you say *a-oo* quickly, you end up with *ow*. A *triphthong* is the same thing with three sounds—put an *ee* on the front of *ow* and you get a *yow* sound.) Many early writers in Australia commented on the resemblance: in 1827, more than sixty years before the *Bulletin* article, the English naval surgeon Peter Cunningham had patronizingly observed that 'even the better sort of them are apt to meet your observation of "A fine day", with their *improving* response of "*Wery* fine indeed!" '[48] Samuel Mossman, around the middle of the century, simpered approvingly over 'the Cockney drawl of the hucksters selling fish and fruit . . . so refreshing to the ear—so thoroughly English,'[49] while in 1891, Edward Kinglake commented that the voices he heard on his expedition to Australia were 'almost identical with the Cockney twang.'[50]

It was unavoidable that the influx of convicts should have a marked effect on the way English developed in Australia. The most reliable modern figure is that just over 160,000 young men and women, with an average age of about 26, made the one-way trip between 1788 and 1868. It is estimated that in 1831 around three-quarters of the population of Australia were either serving convicts or the children of convicts.

But it's less obvious that the convicts' influence would have been specifically Cockney. Sidney Baker, one of the most respected writers on the history of Australian English, views the supposed Cockney pedigree as little more than a myth. There are similarities between the vowel sounds of Cockney and Australian, but there are also important differences between the two accents—Australians have no glottal stop, for instance, they have much slower speech rhythms, and the intonations in the different accents are completely different. In fact, although court records suggest that something over a quarter of all the convicts shipped to Australia came from London and the towns of south-eastern England, another 24 per cent, or over 38,000, were from Ireland, and there are clear Irish influences to match the echoes of

187

Cockney in *kike* and *gripes*. The pronunciation *haitch* is still generally used in Australia for the letter *h*, rather than the *aitch* which is found in New Zealand, North America and most of Britain. Similarly, the Irish pronunciation *youse* is still often found—as in the phrase *I was zony sane lar snite we oughter seeyas*. At most, the native Londoners among the unfortunate and unwilling first Australians would have provided one element among many that would combine over the decades to form the Australian accent.

What happened in Australia was that a whole range of regional accents and dialects was thrown together into the mix. The convicts were overwhelmingly from towns rather than rural areas—some estimates put the ratio at about five to one—and they were almost exclusively working-class. Nearly half of them came from the south-east of England or from various parts of Ireland, but there would also have been accents from virtually every part of England, Wales and Scotland as well.

There had never been such a random mixture of accents before. There were no individual settlements made up overwhelmingly of settlers from a particular region, as there had been on the east coast of America, and there were no social gradations among the convicts. The only comparison is with the movement out into the American West, when settlers from different communities were similarly thrown into close contact with each other—but even in the West, there were some accents that were considered more socially acceptable than others. In the early days of Australia, everyone was equal in misery. There was no single 'educated' or 'correct' accent to which people could aspire.

But that didn't mean that their accents stayed the same. There is a natural tendency for any differences in the way people speak to each other to be reduced over time. Children, in particular, will rapidly acquire accents that are similar to those of the people they meet—about a hundred years after the convicts arrived, the *Sydney Telegraph* described how a group of Second World War evacuees broadcast home to their parents in 1942. Two years earlier, the paper said, 'thick Yorkshire, Scottish, Cockney and East Anglian accents were heard. Tonight, the voices were Australian in tone and idiom.' There was by then, of course, an established and settled accent for these children of the 1940s to copy—but their predecessors of the nineteenth century would have been just as anxious to fit in with other children. A new nation was being born, and by the 1860s, there were as many people living in Australia who had been born there as there were first-generation immigrants. It seems likely that by then, they would have had their own Australian accent.

The effects of the unique mixing of

189

different influences which created that accent continue today, in the similarity of the Australian English spoken in the different regions of the country. Many natives of Victoria often merge their *a* and *e* sounds, so that *salary* and *celery* sound virtually the same, while North Queenslanders are said to have developed a final *-eh?* which ends their sentences, but there are even fewer significant regional variations in Australian English than there are in the United States. Generally, although it is true that accents tend to be broader in the more remote areas and less pronounced in the cities, you can't tell whereabouts in Australia somebody comes from just by listening to their voice in the way that it is possible to tell a Yorkshireman from a Welshman, or even a Texan from a Californian. That isn't to say that all Australians sound the same: a study of more than 9,000 recordings led a research team from Sydney's Macquarie University to suggest three types of Australian English, distinguished by their vowel sounds.[51] The most common one, which the researchers labelled General Australian on the same model as General American, is the accent of the vast majority of Australians, familiar round the world thanks to programmes such as *Neighbours*. Broad Australian, probably the most distinctive way of speaking and the way that inspired the creation of Strine, has longer diphthongs, so that the long *i*-sound which the *Sydney Bulletin* noted so disapprovingly in *cake* is much more pronounced; while Cultivated Australian, which is much closer to British RP and which used to be common among public figures, is now spoken by fewer than 10 per cent of the population.

The popularity of Strine didn't stop Australians from beating themselves up about the way they spoke. More than thirty years after the appearance of *Let Stalk Strine*, the Melbourne-born comedian Barry Humphries observed that, standing in Sydney, he felt 'stranded among people who could not muster the glottal energy to pronounce the *d* in the name of their own city.'[52] Humphries was being testy rather than accurate, as those who criticize other people's speech often are: the *d* he was looking for comes from the front of the mouth, not the glottis. Try to pronounce it with 'glottal energy', whatever that may be, and you stand a very good chance of throttling yourself with your own vocal cords. But the habit of blaming one of the most athletic nations in the world for being too idle to speak their own language dies hard—and no doubt a number of young Australians would have been conscious of the irony of being lectured about physical laziness by a man who makes his living by dressing up in a frock.

The one thing which practically anybody in Britain can tell you about Australian English today is that it is responsible for what is dismissively known as Upspeak or Australian Rising Intonation—the habit of ending sentences with a questioning, upward intonation? Everybody knows that this trick of speech, which annoys people in much the same way as split infinitives or sentences started with 'And', has been popularized by Australian TV soap operas such as *Neighbours*. In fact, *Neighbours* isn't wholly to blame: language doesn't work like that. Rising intonation has been a feature of several versions of English not just in Australia, but also in the West Country, New Zealand, Canada and the United States for generations. Why it should have become popular, especially among young people, in the last few years it is impossible to say, but the fact that it has spread so fast not just in Britain but also among American youngsters, who have much less exposure to Australian soaps, suggests that other factors apart from *Neighbours* may be at work.

What is certain is that its popularity among young people in the last few years has been matched by a storm of grumbling and harrumphing from older English speakers— just the sort of people, in fact, who might be annoyed by the popularity of Australian soap operas. Raising the intonation at the end of a sentence which is not a question 'gives the impression of a weak, indecisive, and immature person,' says one American speech-trainer. Others in Britain describe the habit as 'a real credibility killer,' and warn that women in particular 'will not be taken seriously' if they speak like that. It all seems slightly out of proportion—a bit like the anger induced by those split infinitives, in fact—and it misses the rather more interesting point that intonation is used in much more subtle ways than is usually understood.

The classic model is to say that the intonation of a sentence goes down at the end of a statement, and up at the end of a question—*I am going to the shops* (down) and *Are you going to the shops?* (up). It can turn a sentence which is grammatically a statement into one which will be understood as a question—*You're serious?* In effect, it is the audible equivalent of a question mark. But it's slightly more complex than that. The simple use of an upward inflection is most common in straightforward yes/no questions: if someone were to say *Are you going to town? And what are you going to do there?* the inflection would be unambiguously up at the end of the first sentence, but either neutral or down at the end of the second, which asks for more information. Or consider the sentence *What do you think?* With a simple upward final intonation, it asks for an immediate answer—but with a neutral or downward inflection, it invites a pause for reflection. Put a stress on the word *you* and maintain that neutral or downward inflection, and you have a challenge—in fact, depending on the strength of the stress, you might find yourself in a fight. The distinctions of meaning carried by different intonations can be very subtle. It's almost impossible to write them down on paper, and still more so to try and formulate rules about them. Some people are better at them than others—that's one thing that makes a great actor. Jeremy Paxman can draw out the single word *yesssss* until it has the length, strength and inevitability of a boa constrictor winding itself around his victim and asking, 'Why is this bastard lying to me?' We are not all Jeremy Paxman—but any English speaker can express, say, anger, disbelief, or fear through the intonation of a sentence.

Trying to write down these shades of meaning makes the distinctions sound inflexible. Emily Post, the fearsome New York matriarch who laid down the rules on how to behave for a generation of nervous young men and women, warned in her 1922 book on social etiquette that mistakes should not be made when performing introductions.[53] The younger person should always be presented to the older, rather than vice versa, an unmarried lady to a married one, and a gentleman to a lady—except, she helpfully points out, in the case of the President of the United States, a cardinal or a reigning monarch. But it is not just a matter of choosing the right words: 'The more important name is said with a slightly rising inflection, the secondary as a mere statement of fact,' she declares.

So it is clear that using a rising inflection at the end of a statement, wherever it originally came from, is not carelessly breaking some firm rule of speech and grammar, but simply using one of a whole range of different means of expression. Using it depends on the effect you are seeking: no doubt it is particularly useful when introducing a friend to the President of the United States, a cardinal or a reigning monarch, but its slightly diffident and questioning air may not be the best way to impress your employer with your dynamism and determination when you are looking for a pay rise. It is, in its way, a rather friendly gesture, a bit like a hand held out to be shaken. Generally, an upward inflection breaks up a narrative in the same way that occasional questions like *Do you see what I mean?* or *Are you following me?* might do. (In Queensland, as we've noted, the same effect is achieved with an *eh?* at the end of a sentence. New Zealanders have the same habit—and so, in the northern hemisphere, do many Channel Islanders.) It asks for confirmation or agreement in a less direct way than a simple question. Like most changes in language, its current popularity started out among young people—one survey in Australia estimated that it was used three times as often among people under 21 years old as among older adults. The world is generally less hierarchical and more concerned with reaching consensus than it used to be, and that is even more true among young people.

But the important thing is that the rising inflection fills a role. That is why people adopt it: it helps them to make themselves understood. That, after all, is overwhelmingly the most common reason for languages to change.

* * *

Europeans and Americans may confuse Australian and New Zealand accents— Australians and New Zealanders never do. New Zealanders would point out acidly that they lack the convict background that has done so much to create Australian English, while Australians might mockingly imitate the New Zealanders' pronunciation of *fush and chups*. In fact, New Zealanders, and South Africans too, have experienced their own vowel shift, with the *i* of *fish and chips* moving to *uh*, and *eh* as in *eggs* to *i*. If you're lucky, you may get *iggs for brickfist*. There is also a difference in the vowel sound in words such as *fancy* or *dance*, where most New Zealanders would typically use a long vowel, as in *father*, compared to the short one of an Australian.

The differences partly reflect the different

colonization histories of the two countries. The original settlers in New Zealand came from Australia in the late eighteenth century— although at such an early date, it seems unlikely that they would have been speaking with a distinctively Australian dialect. Many of the flood of newcomers who joined them after British and Maori chieftains signed their peace treaty at Waitangi in 1840 also came from Australia, but others came from all over the British Isles and from America as well. The mix of immigrant accents was comparable to that which poured into Australia, which explains why the two accents are similar—but there were also important differences, which explains why they are not the same.

As free settlers rather than convicts, the new inhabitants of New Zealand were able to choose where they lived, and consequently some opted to set up settlements like the early ones in North America, overwhelmingly populated by people from a particular region. Place names in the far south of the country, such as Invercargill, Dunedin and Stewart Island, reflect the arrival there of large numbers of Scottish and Irish settlers, who also left behind them what is known as the 'Southland R'. Whereas most New Zealanders, like most Australians and speakers of British English, would drop the final *r* on a word like *Septemb-uh*, natives of Southland would finish with a truly rhotic Scottish *rr*. They also tend

197

to pronounce the vowel in words like *fancy* or *dance* with a short, Australian-style *a* as in *had*.

While settlers in Australia found small groups of hunter-gatherers scattered across the country with little contact between them and more than 200 distinct languages, the New Zealand Maori had a well-established farming culture, close links between one region and another, and a single language. As a result, a number of Maori words entered the language, particularly those describing the plants and wildlife for which the Europeans had no words of their own. A few other words, such as *tapu*, meaning *forbidden* or *taboo*, and probably borrowed by the Maori from Tongan dialect, entered the mainstream English vocabulary from further afield. Pakeha, the Maori language, seemed to be disappearing early in the last century but over the last thirty years, encouraged and protected by law, it has survived and prospered in New Zealand in a way that the aboriginal languages of Australia have not, and it is likely that it has influenced spoken English in various ways. Maori speech rhythms, for instance, tend to be faster and more staccato than those of English, and there have even been suggestions that the distinctive *eh?* with which many New Zealanders finish a sentence may be related to the Maori *ne?* which is found at the end of words and which means *Isn't it?*

Another change which some observers have

noted is the increasing Americanization of New Zealand English.[54] It is another change driven by youth: words such as *lieutenant, clerk* and *schedule*, once invariably pronounced in the British way as *lefftenant, clark* and *shedule*, are now heard among up to 90 per cent of university students as *loot'nant, clerk* and *skedule*. The globalization of the economy and the media is increasing the influence of American English all over the world, and it seems that New Zealand English, which has fiercely defended its independence from Australia for generations, is now adopting another and even more powerful model.

*   *   *

South Africa, like Australia and New Zealand, was settled by English-speaking immigrants during the nineteenth century. After their first arrival at the Cape in 1806, British settlers brought their language first to the Eastern Cape, then to Natal, and then to Kimberley and the gold mines of the Witwatersrand. There is no reason to suppose that the backgrounds of these original settlers were markedly different from those who travelled to Australia and New Zealand, so the original 'mix' of regional English accents which went together to make up today's South African English would have been much the same—but the environment in which the language developed was very different indeed.

Where the Australian settlers found disparate groups of aborigines speaking a range of different languages, and the New Zealanders found the Maori with their own culture and language, the newcomers in South Africa arrived in a land where there were not only scores of different African dialects spoken by the indigenous people, but also a thriving community of Dutch-speaking Europeans. The original Afrikaner Protestant settlers arrived in the Cape during the second half of the seventeenth century. Most were from what was then the United Provinces (Netherlands), but they also included people from Germany, France and Scotland. Apart from African slaves and indentured labourers, they also imported workers from Malaya and Malagasy, many of whom would also have spoken Afrikaans—the Dutch word for African.

The different groups, particularly the Dutch, had their effect on the development of South African English in the various parts of the country. To this day, English remains the mother-tongue of less than 40 per cent of the people. Generally, the same vowel shift that happened in New Zealand happened also in South Africa, taking *i* to *uh* and *e* to *i*, so that in South Africa you might get more or less the same *fush and chups* and the same *iggs for brickfist* that you might be offered in New

Zealand. *Ay* has moved to *eye*, so that *mate* would sound to a British ear like *mite*, while *ar* and *ow* have also shifted, so that you would leave your vehicle in a *kaw pawk* rather than a *car park*, and if you found someone had blocked your parking space, you might *shahwt ahwt lahwd* with anger, rather than *shouting out loud*.

However, although outsiders often describe the South African accent as a mixture of Australian and British English, and many Americans say they cannot distinguish between South African and British voices, the effect of the other languages has been to create several different regional accents of South African English, largely depending on how large the Afrikaans-speaking population is in a particular area. The most obvious Dutch or Afrikaans influence is the *r* sound, which is produced further back in the mouth in Dutch. A similar almost guttural *r* is found in the Western Cape and other areas with high Afrikaner populations, and traces of it can be found in the English spoken throughout the country. Pronunciations used by black South Africans have been affected by African languages in various ways, among them the lengthening of the *oo* vowel, so that *look* will often sound more like *loook*, while *ar* is often shortened so that *pardon* sounds like *paddin*. There is still a hangover from the apartheid era in the difference between the English of, say, Nelson Mandela or Desmond Tutu, and that of many white South Africans. Mandela, with the regular stresses of his words and the short vowels, so that *we* sounds like *wiy*, and *work* sounds like *wuk*, exhibits few if any of the characteristics of Dutch which white South Africans have inherited—and they, in turn, show very little influence from the African languages which have always surrounded them. The languages, like the races, of South Africa were kept apart for generations. Now that society has changed, it seems likely that within a generation or two, the guttural sound of Afrikaans-influenced English will become less and less common.

The real lesson of all these Southern Hemisphere accents seems to be that there is little point in trying to define one form of English by reference to another. Just as Geordie or West Country English are not debased versions of RP, so Australian English, New Zealand English and South African English, like General American, are not faulty imitations of British English, but versions of the language which have developed in their own right. Strine is a joke, and a good one too, but divergence is not degeneration, and Australian English, like the English spoken in North America, New Zealand, South Africa and the rest of the English-speaking world, is used by people who are just as cultivated, educated and 'correct' as those in the south-east of England. Australian English is spoken, as any visitor to the country is likely to be told more than once, by the usual winners in cricket, rugby or athletics competitions. But then, South Africans and New Zealanders would say much the same about their own varieties of English.

*   *   *

American English—General American—started its development long before the first settlements in Australia, New Zealand or South Africa. The English from which it developed was different in many ways from the language which the first settlers of those countries spoke, so it was only to be expected that it would develop differently. But the English accents which went into the later colonies were very similar to each other—and yet the three accents today are separate and distinctive. The different histories of Australia, New Zealand and South Africa are important in explaining why that should be so—but they are not the whole story. To understand the differences completely, we need to remember the butterfly.

In the early 1960s, a mathematician and meteorologist at the Massachusetts Institute of Technology named Edward Lorenz discovered that the tiniest difference in the original data he used to prepare a computer weather forecast led to huge divergences in the result. In a paper he later delivered to the American Association for the Advancement of Science, he famously summarized his discovery with the suggestion that a butterfly flapping its wings in Brazil could set off a tornado in Texas—an image that is just about the only thing that most people know about chaos theory.

It is that humble butterfly which holds the key to the development of language, not just in the former colonies of what was once the British Empire, but in every accent of English—indeed, in every language in the world. It is hard to think of a better example of chaos theory than the development of language. There have been all sorts of suggestions, ranging from the ingenious to the frankly barmy, to explain why different accents have developed in North America, Australia, New Zealand, South Africa and the rest of the English-speaking world. Australians suffer from pollen in the atmosphere, people from Birmingham talk with their mouths closed because the pollution is so bad, and Americans either speak a pure English inherited from their settler forebears or struggle to speak at all because of the tobacco they chew; South African English is influenced by Dutch and by a whole range of African languages, Australian English by the languages of the aborigines, and New Zealand by that of the Maori. Any or all of the suggestions may be true—but even without them, the languages would still have developed differently.

It is impossible to predict how languages will change. The original mix of accents among the settlers, the indigenous speech of the natives of the country, social effects of new immigration or changes in the organization of society, the establishment of links between different communities—the list of factors that can affect their development is literally endless, and the smallest difference in any one will lead to significant changes over time. Like the butterfly flapping its wings, each individual may have his own apparently tiny effect. It may be interesting to try and pick out specific factors, but the truth is that languages change because they change—and the one thing that is certain is that the way they change in one place is not the way they will change in another.

But if chaos theory explains the development of language, then why isn't language chaos? Why doesn't everyone in Britain speak with a broad regional accent, and why are the most prestigious accents in most English-speaking countries, despite the effects of national pride and independence, the ones that are closest to the Received Pronunciation of southern England? Why don't the different Englishes of the world gradually get further and further apart until New Zealanders can't understand Americans,

Australians need interpreters to talk to South Africans, and the English themselves look at all of them in blank incomprehension?

To a certain extent, the short answer is that they do: languages do split off and separate when different influences gradually take an accent or a dialect away in new directions. Are the pidgins and creoles of the Caribbean, South America and the South Sea Islands forms of English or separate languages in their own right? Certainly a stockbroker in Surrey would be hard-pressed to understand the Gullah speakers of the south-eastern United States when they say *Jih-w us dis day ow-uh daylih bread*. Or what about a road sign outside the town of Kainantu, which is known as the Gateway to the Highlands in Papua New Guinea, urging people not to leave litter: *Kainantu mas kamap gate way long hailans gen. No ken tromwei pipia.* (*Kainantu must* (*mas*) *become* (*kamap—come up*) *gate way long* (*belong*—used to mean *of*) *hailans* (*highlands*) *gen* (*again*). *No ken* (*You cannot*) *tromwei* (*throw away*) *pipia* (*papers*—used to mean *litter*).)[55] That is written in *Tok Pisin* (*Talk Pidgin*), the national language of Papua New Guinea, but it is clearly linked with English. Or, closer to home, when Oliver Mellors looks at Lady Chatterley so lovingly and tells her *Tha mun come one naight ter th'cottage, afore tha goos; sholl ter?*[56] is he speaking English? There are no clear boundaries in language,

206

only fuzzy lines.

At the same time as there are pressures pulling languages apart, though, there are others holding them together. There is so much travel and communication between Britain, Australia, New Zealand, South Africa and the United States for us to be reasonably sure that an Australian will always be able to read a newspaper in Atlanta, or that a South African will never have a problem ordering a pint of beer in Southampton. Inside Britain, there is constant contact between people from different parts of the country bringing accents closer together. But there is another important factor which encourages people to change the way they speak. But that's the subject for the next chapter.

CHAPTER SEVEN

Laying Down the Law
The rules we all know

So far, we've seen how your accent can both pin you down in society and place you on a map. We've looked at the various ways in which history has affected the way people speak English in different parts of Britain and around the world. Your accent can place you in time as well, because of the way languages change through the generations. But however you speak, it often seems as if there is always some self-important busybody around to tell you that you've got it wrong and to spell out the way you ought to do it differently.

That there should be such grumbles is nothing new. For as long as people have spoken to each other, other people have been finding fault with the way they do it. For hundreds of years, there have been tetchy little books railing against mispronunciations, vulgarisms, Americanisms and other sins against the language, a bit like the books on grammar on booksellers' shelves today. The first I have been able to find in English was William Bullokar's *Pamphlet for Grammar* in 1586, but it is absolutely certain that there were others before him—probably one of the first caveman's grunts was a complaint about the way another caveman had grunted. In the eighteenth century, there were complaints about people saying *wimmin* instead of *woe-men* or *fashun* for *fash-i-on*, and about the pronunciations *gor'jus* and *i'unn* for *gorgeous* and *iron*. Or go back another 800 years: the Anglo-Saxons generally pronounced words as they were spelt, so that the word *cnicht*, or *knight*, would have four separate sounds; our rather apologetic two-syllabled *heaven* had the full four-syllable grandeur of *heofonum*. The words have been pared down and streamlined over the centuries—and the one thing you can be sure about is that every change would have been condemned as yet another piece of sloppy speech.

So far, we've looked mainly at the way that language is actually spoken, in Britain and around the English-speaking world—but there is no shortage of experts to tell us how it *should* be spoken. The traditional way in which a lepidopterist [I use the word *lepidopterist* simply because I think it sounds so much more musical than *butterfly-collector*. The word has its own rhythm—Da, di, diddle-dee, two steps up the stairs and a brief scamper down. And isn't it interesting that words which describe enthusiasms are generally so complicated and classical, almost as if the enthusiasts were trying to distinguish themselves from the common herd Philatelists rather than stamp-collectors, speleologists rather than cavers, and oenophiles rather than wine buffs—and how delightful, incidentally, for someone who would be hard-pressed to tell red wine from white in a blind tasting, that oenophile and onanist look so similar.] used to display butterflies was to chloroform them and pin them to a board. Otherwise, they would have wriggled and flapped too much for him to get his pins in—or at least, that was the excuse. Most people today think it is much more rewarding to see butterflies fluttering around gardens, and to catch those magical moments when they pause to sun themselves on a rock in which to study them more closely. Glass cases of dead insects, like transparent mortuaries hanging on the wall, have rather gone out of fashion in modern living-rooms.

Students of language, too, find it simpler to work once the object of their attention is safely chloroformed, dead and still. There are strict rules of Latin grammar, for instance, as I remember from having to write them out dozens of times whenever I got them wrong. Latin can be relied upon to keep still—but languages that we speak every day, like butterflies, wriggle and flap if you try to pin them down.

If they're still alive, languages struggle even if they are written down, but at least the words on a page are easy to see, easy to reproduce, and easy to argue about—especially when compared to the puff of breath that is, after all, all that a spoken word ever amounts to. Even so, making firm rules, even for written language, is a tricky business. Take spelling, for instance: one of the first spelling rules children are taught is '*i* before *e*,' which is simple enough. However, it doesn't cover words like *conceive* or *receipt*, so it needs to be amended. '*I* before *e*, except after *c*'—that seems to cover the problem. Well, yes—until you get to words like *leisure* and *feign*. So then it becomes '*I* before *e*, except after *c*—when the sound is *ee*'. At least it rhymes, which helps to remember it—but there is still one more addition to be made.

> I *before* e, *except after* c,
> *When the sound is* ee . . .
> *Except, if you please*
> *For the little word* seize.

Once you've remembered the rule, you have to start remembering the exceptions and the special cases, which doesn't seem very satisfactory.

Even so, spelling is now more or less fixed. There may be transatlantic arguments over *color* and *colour*, or *sulfur* and *sulphur*; we may not have quite made up our minds about words like *aggrandise* and *aggrandize*, or *acknowledgment* and *acknowledgement*, and crotchety parents may shake their heads

211

ruefully over abominations like 'C U l8er'—but as a general rule, we know what we are trying to do. When we're writing, a mistake is usually fairly identifiable as a mistake.

With the spoken word, it's different: open your mouth, and you're likely to start an argument about how the words you use should be pronounced. Many of these disagreements come down to the difficulty of matching pronunciation to spelling: words that may have been straightforward to read and pronounce hundreds of years ago are now beset with traps for anyone trying to learn the language, because spelling, being set down on paper, changes so much more slowly than pronunciation. All anyone can do if they try to study English in a classroom is sit down with a list of words such as *cough*, *though*, *plough* and *rough* and try to learn them by heart. It's like a cowboy film I saw when I was young and impressionable, in which two characters were about to start a fight with their Bowie knives. As they stood face to face, one of them said, 'We'd better sort out the rules before we start,' at which the other simply kicked him hard and painfully in the crotch. Looking down scornfully at the writhing, gasping figure of the man he'd been about to fight, he grunted, 'Rules? In a knife fight?' and turned away. Think of pronunciation as a knife fight.

And yet, just as in a knife fight, there are rules—but they are rules that everyone knows

212

instinctively. We may not be able to write them down or explain them, but we pick them up without noticing—all of us. If there are people outside a university department of linguistics who understand the Rule of Trisyllabic Shortening, for instance, I have yet to meet them—and yet virtually every mother-tongue speaker of English would obey it without a thought. It states that a stressed long vowel will generally be shortened when it is followed by two other syllables—and even after hearing it, hardly any English speaker in the world would be able to agree or disagree without trying a few examples. What it means is that a word like *divine*, with a long second vowel, becomes *divinity*, with a short one, as soon as a third syllable is added. It still takes a moment or two to get your head round it, but just think *grade*, *gradual*, *serene*, *serenity*, *incline*, *inclination*, or *inane*, *inanity*. We may not know it in the classroom sense that we can recite '*i* before *e*,' but we obey it implicitly.

We are also aware of the one absolutely firm Rule of Language, which trumps even the Rule of Trisyllabic Shortening. It is that there are no absolutely firm rules of language. What about the word *obese*, which doesn't change its vowel sound, and becomes *obesity*? So we know the exceptions as well as we know the rule. But do we obey these rules instinctively? That is a question that would start a whole series of arguments in a roomful of linguistic

213

scholars. Exactly *how* we remember the structures of language, how much is 'hard-wired' into the brain, how much is learned by imitation, how much by reasoning and analogy, and how much by instruction, are all subjects that no three academics would agree about. But then, language excites just as much passion among university experts as it does in the back bar of the Dog and Duck: six rats in a sack would be a model of calm co-operation compared with a roomful of academic linguists. We can argue about how or why people remember these complex rules of pronunciation that nobody knows, but the fact is that they do. It's another reminder that we handle our language with greater subtlety than we are often given credit for.

Take the letter *s*, for instance. It can be pronounced either as a simple hissing sound, as it is in *kiss*, or *mistake*; it can be a *z*-sound, as it is in *kids* or *his*; or it can be a *zh* sound, as in *pleasure* or *lesion*. In the north of England, *us* would generally be pronounced *uz*, while in the south, it would be *uss*—although that shouldn't lead anyone to make a sweeping generalization about how northerners and southerners pronounce their *s*'s, as the word *because* is the other way round. In the north, it's *bicawss*, and in the south, *bicoz*. Anyone learning English from a book might have great difficulty in getting the right sound in the right word, but no one who has learned it naturally,

214

as a child, would ever confuse them.

With other letters, the situation is still more complex. The compliant letter *s*, for all its idiosyncrasies, does not cause any serious problems because there is near-universal agreement about how it is used—although an orthoeptist, or student of pronunciation (another example of a learned word describing an enthusiasm) would point out that the *s* in *kiss* is subtly different from that in *mistake*, that the one in *kids* is not quite the same as the one in *his*, and that the sounds in *pleasure* and *lesion* are completely different—but that just reinforces the point. The vast majority of English accents give a single final *s* a voiced pronunciation which leaves it somewhere between *s* and *z*. However, its alphabetical neighbour, *t* is much more controversial.

Any primary school child, working painstakingly through the alphabet, could tell you that *t* says *tuh*, as in the famous 'two-ton truck taking toilet-tissue to Teddington.' (As a joke, it's not worth repeating, but as an example of tapped *t*'s, it's hard to beat.) It's fairly simple at the start of a word—tapped, to use the technical term, with the tip of the tongue against the alveolar ridge—but in the middle of words like *bottle*, the same letter has a completely different sound. A very young child may talk of a *lickle bockle* or a *litt-ull bott-ull*—Katie Melua, in her song *Market Day in Guernica* adopts a toe-curlingly faux-innocent pronunciation when she sings about *my litt-ull ones*—but in normal speech across most of the United Kingdom, the sound is made by curving the tongue slightly, with the tongue resting on the alveolar ridge, rather than with the spit of a tapped *t*.

But of course, as always, there is a catch. Americans, as we have seen, pronounce an initial *t* much the same as British English speakers, but give it their own distinctive *d* sound in the middle of a word. In fact, for Englishmen in the US, the letter *t* is fraught with peril: a tapped, English-style *t* in the middle of a word like *matter* is one hallmark of stereotypical homosexual speech in America.

So we pick up these tiny distinctions between different ways of speaking the same letter without having to learn any rules to guide us—and by and large, there's little disagreement about them. If anyone in most of Britain talked about *the birdss and the beess*, for instance, with the same sibilant *s*-sound as they would use at the beginning of *silent*, it might mark them out as a foreigner who had not learned English as his mother tongue, but it wouldn't cause any offence. But there are particular habits of speech which seriously get up people's noses.

There is the dreaded glottal stop, of course—the habit that marks the Prime Minister out as really one of the lads. We'll look at that in a later chapter. But even more

216

widespread is the habit of dropping aitches, which seems to have been putting people's backs up for as long as anyone can remember. The fact that the *'orrible 'abit* never spread to America suggests that it wasn't common in England when the first settlers were leaving in the sixteenth and seventeenth centuries, but by the eighteenth century, when the publication of grammar books grumbling about how the language was going to the dogs was at its height, it was clearly very widespread—and not only among the lower classes. The Scottish writer James Elphinston noted in his *Inglish Speech and Spelling under Mutual Guides* in 1787 that 'many Ladies, Gentlemen, and others have totally discarded' the letter *h* from the beginning of their words.

So for a time, *h*-dropping was fashionable—but then, during the nineteenth century, not pronouncing your *h*'s became a social millstone for anyone who wished to move in polite society. As the century began, John Walker's *Pronouncing Dictionary* of 1791 was still widely circulated, with its condemnation of the 'vice' of *h*-dropping. It was, he said, the worst of the bad habits of the people of London—which might suggest to anyone slightly less ill-disposed towards them that they must have been a pretty virtuous lot. A little heavy-handed nineteenth-century humour, incidentally, brought the expression 'to eat humble pie' into the language by putting an *h* on to the front of a separate word, *umbles*, which meant the offal of a deer. So, if you really wanted to be pernickety and drop your *h*'s at the same time, you could quite legitimately refer to eating *umble pie*. By the twentieth century, linguistic scholars were being more analytical—but although the respected Danish linguist Otto Jespersen found several examples of dropped *h*'s that were almost universal throughout the language, he still added that 'others belong to vulgar or dialect speech.'[57] Lost *h*'s, clearly, still meant lost social standing.

They still do—and putting them in where they shouldn't be is even worse. There's a story about a guide in a Lancashire cotton mill museum, who was showing a group of schoolchildren where the wooden bobbins were made on to which the cotton was wound. The different bobbins were made of different woods, he told them—of 'hoak, hash, helm, and 'ornbeam'. Another example of hyper-correction, like the small boy looking in the *mirroh*. That's what happens when a particular habit of speech becomes heavily stigmatized: you can be so keen not to be seen to drop an *h* that you tag them in front of every vowel that you see. Where the usual grumble about other people's use of language is that it's careless, this seems to be a problem caused by being *too* careful—caring too much what other people think.

So misplaced *h*'s are at the very least a potential source of embarrassment. As a very small and innocent boy, I was convinced for months that I was possessed of a word of such profanity that it was almost magical in its power. I guessed that it's initial *h* must have been dropped because that was the way that all the ragamuffins who were daring enough actually to use it spoke. Lying quietly in my bed at night, I would repeat it over and over again to myself as if it were a magic spell that would turn me from a little boy into a strong, macho and devil-may-care hero. Luckily, I found out my mistake before I ever showed how tough I was by saying the word *harse*.

The story of the letter *h* seems to demonstrate that for all the harrumphing about sloppy speech, what's right and what's wrong is usually simply a question of fashion. What was right a few decades ago may be wrong today. But anyone who tries to lay down the law about how words should sound will find that the rules of pronunciation are written in water, not carved in stone. They change not only with the ins and outs of fashion and the passing of the years, but also according to the situation in which people find themselves. Ask how someone pronounces the word *are*, for instance, and in nine cases out of ten you will get the answer *ar*. But if you say *John and Sue ARE having an affair*, you are doing more than just passing on a tasty piece of gossip—you are also meeting head-on the suggestion that they might just be good friends. Say it calmly and expressionlessly, and you end up with *John and Sue uh having an affair*. In the vast majority of sentences, *are* is little more than a grunt: very few people know accurately how they speak.

The most avid phonologist, collecting evidence on how people actually do pronounce their words as opposed to how they say they pronounce them, will admit that there are several different situations which will provide different results. If people are asked to read from a list of words, each one is likely to be enunciated carefully—like the word *are*, for instance. Young children reading aloud and still so unsure that they concentrate on each individual word will read like this, so that the different pronunciations of *the* (*thuh* before a consonant and *thee* before a vowel) come out at random, and each syllable is given equal care, weight and emphasis.

You can often hear the difference on radio and television, where, because broadcasters read out prepared scripts but try to give the impression that they are speaking off-the-cuff, there is an awkward combination of written and spoken English. Talented professionals like John Humphrys or John Simpson can both write a script that sounds like speech and read it so it sounds as if it had just come into their heads, while Melvyn Bragg, on the other hand, generally makes no pretence at all of natural

220

speech as he rushes through the introduction to his *In Our Time* programme. And of course, there are the mistakes caused by lazy announcers not reading their scripts through to themselves before they read them on air— how many listeners have been puzzled by the announcement that traffic is being held up not by a *shed LOAD*, but by *a SHED-load*. A shed-load of what, we wonder.

Often, those who complain about people's pronunciation try to bolster their case by the slightly dishonest technique of spelling out individual words and phrases in order to make them look ridiculous. There was a particular type of political columnist who used to deride Tony Benn's passionate insistence that politics should concentrate on the *ishoos*, as they wrote it. Does anybody in the world pronounce *issues* with an *s* sound as in *stupid*, and a *y* sound before the *oo*? Well, maybe a very few people who have graduated with honours from elocution school, but not enough to make the pronunciation *ishoos* worth commenting on.

When members of the Professional Association of Teachers complained about the standard of speech on BBC Television children's programmes, they too spelt out their grumbles letter by letter. One of the phrases they disliked was, as they put it, *Wotcha want?*—but again, odd as it looks, *wot* pretty well sums up how virtually everyone in

221

England would pronounce *what*. Nobody—even in the Professional Association of Teachers—would ever say *What do you want?* with the initial *h* sound, and the final *t*'s of *what* and *want* carefully enunciated as in *tea*. And the words they mockingly write down are not even an exact reproduction of the sentence as it is spoken: no one, in Britain at least, would say the word *want* with an *a*-sound, so the phonetic version should be something like *wonnt*. The vowel is almost identical with the *o* in *hot*—and, come to that, with the *a* in *what* as well. A more honest way of reproducing the way the vast majority of people speak would be to write the sentence *Wo' d'yoo wont?* or even *Wo' j'oo won'?* Not as extreme a change as *Wotcha want?* perhaps, but still a shortened version of the original, written sentence. And it's hard to see why one contraction should be more acceptable than another.

There were also complaints about *Wassup?*, which they suggested should be replaced by *What are you doing?* It would, presumably, have been too ridiculous for even these po-faced guardians of the language to suggest that children's television announcers should solemnly demand *What is up?*—but that is the grammatical and colloquial expression they are complaining about. Again, they've got it wrong anyway—what they should really have written, if they want to mimic the sound of the word, is *Wossup?* And in any case, the *t* of *It's*

222

is often elided in spoken English, as in the sentence *Well, I think 's a stupid complaint*, so *Wassup?* doesn't seem to be such a gross dereliction of the presenters' duty. Once again, the teachers were simply trying to make their complaint sound more convincing by cobbling together a supposedly phonetic version of a perfectly ordinary spoken expression.

But speech is not writing—something that the teachers might consider writing out a hundred times after school. We all drop consonants, elide words and syllables, and shift vowels with a much more casual abandon than we would ever admit. Take the word *grandfather*. A few old buffers might still insist on it as a term of respect, as mine did years ago, on the grounds that *granddad* is too childish, and *grandpa*—in his view at least—simply rude. But very few, if any, would think to insist on that middle *d* in any of them. If we remember the fuss that a dropped *h* can cause, it seems ironic that a *d* can vanish with nobody even noticing it—but it does. And there are more unnoticed changes going on than that: we say—or at least the vast majority of us do—*gran'father, gran'dad*, and—well, not *gran'pa*. The spelling makes you *think* you say *gran'pa*, but the sound that comes out, for most English speakers, would be *gram'pa*. The reason is simple: an *n* is pronounced with the tongue on the alveolar ridge, while an *m* is pronounced with the lips, like the *p*. Going from *n* to *p* is harder work than going from *m* to *p*, and so we automatically and unconsciously substitute the easier pronunciation for the more complex one. Lazy speech, a pedant would insist—but a more helpful analogy might be the working of an efficient machine. We don't work for the language: we make the language work for us.

But to do that, we have to learn to have a bit of confidence in ourselves. It's *our* language, after all—and the so-called experts don't always know best. Dictionaries, for instance, will give dates for the first known use of a particular word, which can be interesting and revealing as far as they go—the word *scientist* isn't listed before 1840, for instance. And isn't it interesting that an obviously newfangled word like *newfangled* was being bandied about by grumpy old men in the fourteenth century?—but they tell you very little about the real age of the word. In most cases, it will have been used for years as part of the spoken language before it finds its way into print and under the spotlight of the dictionary. And looking for guidance about the way we should speak words from the way we read them on the page is even more risky.

Everybody knows, for instance, that English has five vowels, *a, e, i, o* and *u*. Some people, suspecting a trick question, might say six, and point out words like *cyst* or *lyric* where *y* does the job of a vowel. The really suspicious might think of the Welsh word *cwm*, which describes

224

a bowl-shaped rocky depression in the mountains, and wonder whether inclusion in the Oxford English Dictionary means that an ancient Celtic word qualifies as English, and sneaks in *w* as a seventh. But those quibbles aren't the point: what the question highlights is the confusion between letters and sounds, between written and spoken English.

In fact, most people would miss the most useful and common vowel of all, the one without which language would grind to a halt. Indeed, the vast majority would never even have heard of *schwa*, though they may use it fifty times in a sentence. Sherlock Holmes, lecturing the patient Watson on how easy it is to break most codes, pointed out that *e* is by far the commonest letter in the English language, which is perfectly true as long as you are talking about writing. Once you turn to the spoken language, however, there is no sound that comes anywhere near schwa for popularity. It's the word linguists use for a lightly-pronounced, unaccented syllable, which sounds very like the *uh* which a child would say was the sound made by *u*. The catch is that it can be represented by any of the five standard vowel-letters, and by a lot of other combinations as well: in most dialects, the final syllable of *after* or *brother* would be a schwa, or you could find it in *adept* with an *a*, in *synthesis* with an *e*, in *decimal* with an *i*, in *ignominy* with an *o*, or in *medium* with a *u*. Even *y* doesn't escape—think of *syringe*.

*   *   *

Most languages have a range of between fifteen and seventy-five distinctive sounds— the Piraha people of the Brazilian Amazon struggle by with only ten, while the Ixoo language spoken in Botswana and Namibia has around 140, including a variety of different clicks. Depending on how you count, English is fairly well-stocked with around forty-four. There are about twenty distinct vowel sounds—think of the words *reed, rid, red, radish, card, cod, cord, cooed, cud, curd, fade, fight, foil, foam, pounce, peer, pair, poor* and *put.* That's an unusually high number, compared with other languages—some, like Greek, Spanish and Japanese, have only five— and it helps to account for the difficulty many foreigners have in learning to speak English. And of course, each of these distinct sounds can be pronounced in various ways, depending on what part of the country or what part of the world you are in. *Boat*, for instance, may have a pure, simple *oh* sound, or it may have a long drawn out *oh-a; fight* may have a simple *eye-* diphthong, or it may be opened out almost as far as *fay-ut*. Most of the time, we know without thinking whether a shift in sound implies a shift in meaning, or whether it is simply an alternative pronunciation: we are

226

cleverer than we think—which is another central message of this book. Children learning to speak have usually mastered the lot before they are 2½.

There are about twenty-four consonants—think of the twenty-six letters of the alphabet, and subtract the five vowels. Of the twenty-one consonants left, the sounds of *c, q* and *x* are all duplicated by other letters, giving a total of eighteen distinct alphabetical consonants. Then there are six other consonant sounds—*ch* as in *church, th* as in *though, th* as in *thin, ng* as in *sing, zh* as in *leisure*, and *sh* as in *ship*. It can only be an approximate list, as there are slight differences in the sounds of many of the consonants depending on where they are in a word—remember *kill, cull* and *cool*—but it is the consonants which generally cause children more trouble. They are simply harder to produce than vowels—whereas the vowel sounds are formed with a free flow of air from the lungs, pronouncing consonants involves blocking the flow in some way, either with the lips or the tongue. A whole new series of muscles comes into play.

The differences between the movements needed for the various consonants may be tiny but crucially significant, and they are often coupled with variations in the strength of the airflow. Try to describe the distinction between *tuh*, where your tongue is close to your front teeth, and *duh*, where it is further back in your mouth, and you would probably never get the hang of it: simply copy your parents doing it, and you can manage it before your first birthday. It's fortunately true that *duh* and *muh* are among the first sounds babies make—enabling parents to celebrate the fact that, when their new babies say *mumumumum* or *duhduhduhduh*, they are, quite obviously, really saying *Mummy* and *Daddy*. A linguistic student might say that they were mastering their nasals and plosives, which seems somehow less exciting. Other consonants may be even trickier—the different-sounding *t* in the middle of *little*, which is made around the edges of the tongue, can take a lot longer to learn, so that children typically say either *litt-ull* or *lickle*. They are often 5 years old before they have stopped saying *w* for *r*—*wabbit* for *rabbit*—and sometimes 8 before they can manage *thing* instead of *fing*. Some children also say *f* for *tr*, which can be embarrassing when they are pointing out a truck.

The significance of all this is that it is learned in an entirely natural way. There are constant arguments about the best way to teach a child to read—to translate the symbols on the page into the sounds he recognizes—but speaking is learned almost entirely by example. Learning a second language as an adult is an entirely different process, and seldom as successful. However well they master the new grammar and structure, adults will generally carry habits of pronunciation from their first language across into their second.

The catch for doting parents is that they have little control over what example their child will follow. Some people, like the government minister Hilary Benn, may inherit certain habits from their parents—Benn's rounded vowels could only have come from his father, Tony Benn—but the most important influence on the way children speak is not their parents, but their peer group. We speak, in other words, like the people we want to be like—and that, for those who can't remember their own childhood, emphatically generally does not mean our parents. Tony Benn should be flattered. There are many parents who spend large sums of money paying for their children to go to the sort of schools where they should pick up a 'correct' accent, only to find that they come home talking like a *Big Brother* housemate.

The real issue, pedants will usually tell you, is clarity: in just the same way that an errant apostrophe on a greengrocer's counter causes them to demand petulantly 'A tomato's *what?*', dropping an *h*, they tell you, can transform the meaning of a sentence. Whether this is true is another matter—it is unlikely that anyone has ever genuinely misunderstood the sentence *I 'ate my mother-in-law*—but every now and then, there is a genuine confusion between words that sound the same—*homophones*. Anyone who heard Jimi Hendrix performing *Purple Haze* in the 1960s might have needed an intimate knowledge of his sexual preferences to know whether he was singing about kissing the sky or 'this guy'. The American tourist who, clearly over-impressed by the pageantry of the Houses of Parliament, fell reverently to his knees when he heard someone calling the first name of the then Labour leader, Neil Kinnock, may have been naïve, but he wasn't deaf—there's no difference between *Neil* and *kneel*. And President Bush's Texan drawl might sometimes leave people wondering whether the United States is targeting *world terrorism* or *world tourism*.

Or there was the unfortunate boat race commentator on the radio who, after a very BBC 'Oh, I say' kind of appreciation, allegedly told a fascinated nation, 'Isn't that nice! The wife of the Cambridge president is kissing the cox of the Oxford eight!' It was hardly his fault—or hers—if he was misunderstood.

Such mix-ups, however, hardly ever exist in real life: people generally understand what is said to them almost as much because of the meaning and context as because of the actual sound of the words. For most speakers, the pronunciation of *workman* is exactly the same as that of *workmen*—it's only the context that makes it clear whether you are expecting one man with a shovel or a whole gang of them. Similarly, the point of Ronnie Barker's famous sketch, where he comes into a hardware shop and is given the 'four candles' that he appears to have asked for, and then has to explain that what he really wants is 'fork 'andles', is that there is no context to guide the meaning. 'I'd like some candles, please—four of them,' or, 'I'd like some fork 'andles,' would have spoiled the sketch, but avoided the confusion.

Sometimes, the confusion of similar-sounding words can be a source of pointed humour. Solomon Binding was a famous character in 1970s trade union negotiations, with his eponymous agreements between managements and workers; Conservative politicians were conducting passionate and highly publicized affairs with Laura Norder long before John Major started his Back to Basics campaign. And how wonderful for anyone disenchanted with the growth of official curiosity about our private lives, that the BBC should repeatedly refer to the Pry Minister, Tony Blair. There are those who believe that President Bush reveals his hidden agenda every time he talks about America's *noo-killer* deterrent. And for people in Britain who look forward to a chilly and poverty-stricken retirement, there are frequent news reports about the government's Stay-Colder Pension Schemes—not to mention the famous humanitarian physician, N. A. Chess, or the region where one can expect to be seriously ripped off, at least as far as property prices are concerned, South E Sting-Land. And in *Martin Chuzzlewit*, Charles Dickens introduces The Lord No Zoo.

But the point is that the speakers of a language establish for themselves what degree of confusion is acceptable and what is not. Underlying all the linguistic changes, the missing sounds and slurred syllables, however they may simplify the way people speak, is the fact that the whole purpose of language is communication. If people don't understand, then there's no point in talking.

*   *   *

So the spoken language is different. Not only is it constantly evolving, from one generation to the next, more quickly than writing, but there are differences from one region to another, and one class to another. If a Yorkshireman tells you to put the tea in the cup, it will sound different from the way a Londoner will tell you, and different again from a West-countryman. A barrow-boy and a brigadier are unlikely to sound the same. But there is no unchallenged authority to which people could turn if they wanted to describe one pronunciation as right and the other as wrong: the language is not so much wriggling as in a state of perpetual motion. If the

English that we speak is different from that of our grandfathers, we can be sure that the English our grandchildren speak will be very different again.

CHAPTER EIGHT

Picking Up Tab Ends
How language changes

My old maths teacher had a standard joke which he always used to tell his new first-year pupils. Teachers, he would say with a warning look around the room over the top of his glasses, always knew what their nicknames were. In his case, he said, he didn't understand why he had been given the name, but he knew he was called Zeer—simply because whenever he approached a classroom, he could hear dozens of small boys hissing to each other, 'Zeer, Zeer, Zeer!'

It was about as funny as teachers' jokes usually are—but it helps to explain one crucial way in which words and pronunciations change. The different sounds which make up a word or a sentence have to fight to survive: the ones which don't seem important, or which are simply too much trouble to say, just get dropped. Some, like the old ½p coin which used to clutter our pockets, are just not worth keeping. No doubt most of the boys in the maths lessons, even at 12 years old, would have known to *write* the sentence 'He is here!' but, whispering it one to another as they scrambled to get back to their places, stick their chewing gum under the desk, hide their comics and open their maths books, they simply lost the initial 'He i . . .' in their panic. ' 'Zeer, 'zeer, 'zeer!'

Things like that are happening all the time, as the language slowly changes shape. The tiny individual developments of a few decades—the shift in the meaning of *cool*, for instance, or the *eh*-sound of Mrs Van Hopper's *a*'s in the film *Rebecca* in 1940—may not seem much, but together, over hundreds of years, they transform the way English is spoken. Letters, syllables, even whole words and phrases vanish like food in a blender as our sentences turn into a sort of easily-digestible audible porridge. It can seem odd in print—*moffrabeer* or *wairjasayzgohn?* look like the sort of alphabet soup you get in Swahili or Polish, but they are a pretty fair representation of how many people would say *I'm off for a beer* and *where do you say he's going?*

This pruning of syllables may cause exquisite mental agony to the sort of people who complain that *Wednesday* is increasingly being pronounced *Wensdy*, or to those who cringe when their teenage children ask them, *It's orright, innit?* But even the fussiest speaker will generally pronounce *Wednesday* with only two syllables rather than its full three, and with at best a brief half-stop at the front of his mouth in the middle of the word rather than a 'proper', well-formed, *d*—and it would be

235

tricky to explain why it is all right to turn 'Is it not?' into 'Isn't it?', as virtually every speaker of English would do, but a sin against language, morality and all the laws of civilized behaviour to take it one step further and say 'Innit?'

Generally, the sounds that vanish as languages change and develop are the unstressed ones. You can see it in children when they are learning to speak—a banana may become a *'nana*, for instance, or a potato a *'tato*. Adults do much the same: *February* is under attack on two fronts, with some people saying *Febr'y* and others *Febuary*. In its way, it's a bit like Jonathan Swift's battle between those who opened their eggs at the big end, and those who chose the little end—whichever side wins, the old-style four-syllable *February* is almost certainly doomed. Either the *u* or the *r* is on the way out. In the same way, *interesting* has almost universally become *int'r'sting*, and *probably* is rapidly turning into *prob'ly*. The only way to tell is to listen as people actually speak: if you ask someone how they pronounce the word *probably*, they will almost always carefully spell it out syllable by syllable. Listen to them put it in a sentence when they are not thinking about it, though—when they think no one is looking—and the most you are likely to hear is a slight pause on the *b*.

Similarly, you'll hear more and more people taking about *vi'l'nce* rather than *violence*.

These contractions are annoying at first, then accepted in practice but not in theory, and finally completely assimilated into the language—it's worth noting that though people may complain about the loss of the middle *o* syllable of *violence*, for instance, it has in any case been on its way out for years, along with the *eh* in the syllable that follows it. At any time in the last century, only the prissiest speaker would have spoken of *vi-oh-lence* rather than *vi-uh-lunce*. The descent to that generalized *uh* sound is often the first sign that a syllable is dying—the first headache, so to speak, or a slight rise in temperature. That particular contraction has long been absorbed into the language so that it attracts no notice, but the further change from *viol'nce* to *vi'l'nce* may still have some way to go before it is completely accepted.

All these examples, of course, are as subjective as most descriptions of how language is changing. That's *what* happens—language and the way we speak it is liquid, not solid. It constantly changes its shape. But that still doesn't explain *how* it happens. Language has changed so much and so subtly, with the effects of regional accents, random fashions and the energetic work of 'reformers' of various sorts, that it will never be possible to fix on a universally-accepted chain of cause and effect.

But we can still see some general trends,

and the image I referred to earlier of the comatose teenager, slumped dozily in front of the television, as the unresting motor of linguistic progression, is central to them. By and large, it is young people who start the changes. For a start, there are deliberate new pronunciations which come and go among teenagers with such speed that merely writing them down is almost a guarantee that they will be out of date. There may be no reason for them other than that they are different: if older people complain about them, then they might have served their purpose. They are not only idiosyncratic, but also exclusive: anyone in their thirties or forties—even David Cameron—might just about get away with describing things as 'wicked' (meaning, of course, 'wonderful') or 'cool' (meaning, naturally, 'pretty hot') if they wanted to, but daring to imitate the teenage pronunciation of a couple of years ago of *wick-ID* or *coo-ULL* would have drawn the ultimate condemnation of eyes raised to the skies and a surly murmur of 'So embarrassing!' And quite right too.

One of the main ways in which pronunciation changes is in the passing of language from one generation to another. Children will instinctively adopt the version they hear from their parents and then build in their own minor adaptations, developed as they talk with their friends. Vowels gradually change in this way as years go by. The long *o*

238

with which anyone in the eighteenth century would have pronounced the word *stomach* has mutated into the *uh* with which we say the word today. When children talk about their *tummy*, the initial *s* has gone, there is a friendly little *-my* instead of the final syllable, and the vowel is written as it is spoken. For the most part, the changes are so gradual as to be imperceptible, but slowly and inexorably, in speech as in everything else, the younger generation gets its way. The catch is, of course, that eventually it becomes the old generation and has to grumble in its turn as its own changes to the language are superseded. What goes around comes around.

But the most crucial thing is that we should be understood. When the way people speak has shifted over the centuries as much as it has, it is inevitable that some sounds that were once clearly different from each other should have become impossible to tell apart. For most British English speakers, *meet* sounds like *meat, grown* like *groan*, or *side* like *sighed*. Some dialects with different vowel sounds may have different areas of confusion—there is a famous story about a young boy in Yorkshire who is found sobbing by the side of a river.

'What's the matter?' a passer-by asks him, and he's shocked when the boy tells him, 'Me mate's fallen in t'watter.' 'How did that happen?' he asks, as he turns to call an ambulance—and the boy replies, 'I dunno. It

239

just slipped from between t'slices o' bread.'

Well, it's a better example than it is a joke.

*　　　*　　　*

The favourite phrase of the people who want to tell us how to speak, whether they are talking about our pronunciation or our grammar, is 'Well, it's just not English!' Sometimes they'll sniff grumpily that *sye-multaneous* rather than *simmultaneous*, or *nooz* instead of *news*, are just Americanisms, as if that ended the argument. But the language itself is nothing like so prissy. English has always picked up words, phrases and pronunciations wherever it could find them, like a tramp scooping up old tab ends in the gutter. All languages do that, but English, partly because of the Norman invasion of 1066, partly because of Britain's imperial past, and partly because of the way the language has spread around the world, seems to do it more than most.

There is an old story, which ought to be true even if it isn't, of an Englishman being regaled by a Scottish friend with the long and convoluted history of his clan, the battles it had won and the tartan it traditionally wore. Eventually, the Englishman let slip that he, too, was thinking of buying a kilt. 'Ah didnae ken that ye had the right tae wear the kilt,' said the Scotsman. 'Have ye Scottish blood?'

'Oh no,' said the Englishman, who probably came from Yorkshire. 'But I was born in England, so I wear what the hell I choose.'

If you come from Yorkshire, you'll probably think he was quite right; if you don't, you'll probably think he was a pompous bastard. Both may be true, of course—but the point is that the English language has the same attitude to foreign words that the Yorkshireman had to the kilt. It just assumes the right to try them on, pull them around here and there a bit to make them fit, and then quietly adopt them as its own.

That process of making them feel right can go on for hundreds of years. Foreign words are gradually absorbed into the language, like jetsam on the sea bed being slowly coated in coral. As traders, soldiers, colonists and now shoppers and holidaymakers have carried English round the globe, they have brought back new words and phrases into the language. Foreign names, foreign spellings and foreign sounds are gradually anglicized, until the word is more in line with the rest of the English vocabulary. One generation's mistakes and incomprehension become the unquestioned correctness of the next. Maybe it's significant, considering the number of tax-free shopping trips that are made there, that English people today travel to *Do-buy* or even *D'you-buy?* in the Gulf, rather than to the Arabic *D'bay*. Its neighbouring city-state, Abu Dhabi, loses the gentle liquid Arabic *dh* halfway between *d* and *th*, to become simply *Aboo Dabby*.

Similar adaptations have been going on for centuries. In 711 AD, the Arab general Tariq ibn-Ziyad led his armies into Spain, and landed on a rocky promontory just across the straits from North Africa. He gave the huge rock (*jebel* in Arabic) on which he landed his own name, so it became Jebel Tariq—which, allowing for the changes between three languages and nearly 1,300 years as it metamorphosed from Arabic to Spanish and from Spanish to English, is what Gibraltar remains today. The final *-iq* has vanished partly because it is an unstressed syllable, but also because the guttural Arabic *q* is hard for a westerner to pronounce. Elsewhere in Spain, the Arabs found a great river running out into the Gulf of Cadiz. With more precision than imagination, they named it simply The Great Valley, or *Wadi al Kabir*—which, if you remember that if you say a *v* with your lips together, you get a *b*, is just recognizable today as the Guadalquivir River.

And, of course, it doesn't just happen with Arabic words. The Jerusalem artichoke no more comes from Jerusalem than Roman candles come from Rome, or German measles from Germany. It's a species of sunflower with an edible root, which turns to face the sun as it grows—*girasole*, as the Italians who sold it to English merchants in the early seventeenth century would have said. Whether the merchants misunderstood or whether they simply thought that *Jerusalem* would be a tempting brand-name for their merchandise is not known, but *girasole* became *Jerusalem* on the journey over from Italy, and has stayed so ever since.

There are occasional problems about this: the innocent enjoyment of an avocado salad may be compromised by the knowledge that the word *avocado* comes originally from the South American Nahuatl word *ahuacatl*, which means testicle, particularly since you only have to look at an avocado to understand why. On the other hand, there is a certain amiable pleasure to be gained from the fact that the leaves of the dandelion look like the teeth of a lion—or, as they might say in France, *les dents de lion*, even though the French themselves, aware of the plant's diuretic properties, call it rather less poetically *le piss-en-lit*, or the piss-a-bed.

But taking a word into English can involve more changes than the simple misrepresentation of an unfamiliar foreign sound. The English word *apron*, for instance, started its life in English sometime around the fourteenth century as a *naperon*, a straight borrowing from French, but within two hundred years—its unstressed middle syllable, incidentally, having been eroded away—it was being written indiscriminately as *a napron* and *an apron.* By the end of the seventeenth century, *napron* was no longer seen, and the word had completed its absorption into English, with its initial *n* now firmly attached to the indefinite article in front of it. Similarly, the word *orange* traces its history back through the mediaeval Italian *narancia* to the Arabic *naranj*, and ultimately the Sanskrit *naranga*. The Spanish still use *naranja*, but by the time it had reached French, and then English, the word had lost its *n*, to become, not *a norange* but *an orange.* The same process can work in a different way, by bundling two words together: the Arabic word *jbr*, for example, meant literally 'the resolution of problems'. That's a fairly romantic way to describe doing sums, but the expression, coupled with *al*, the Arabic word for *the*, was taken into thirteenth-century English as *al-jbr*, or *algebra.* Later writers in English imaginatively suggested that the word had been coined in homage to a fourteenth-century Arab alchemist, Jabir, whose name was westernized as Geber—but it was simply an anglicized version of the Arab word for getting the right answer. Much the same process produced words like *alchemist, alcohol, apricot* and *almanac.*

Words don't even have to cross from one language to another to be reconstructed in this way. One famous English example is *nickname*, which comes from the Anglo-Saxon phrase *eke-name. Eke* meant 'also', so an *eke-*

244

name was simply an alternative name given to someone—but by the sixteenth century, the *n* from *an eke-name* had been sucked into the word. The process is called rebracketing, but the most important aspect of it for anyone interested in pronunciation is that it shows how the way a word is spoken can affect the way it is written down. The argument, as we've seen already, is usually the other way round— 'This is how it is spelled, so this is how it should be pronounced'—but the history of aprons, oranges, nicknames and algebra is a useful reminder that, while the written word may seem to be more permanent than speech, the way words are spoken can also decide the shape of the language.

It's possible to take this principle too far. In *Nicholas Nickleby*, Dickens's Wackford Squeers, who called a *window* a *winder*, had no hesitation about explaining to his pupils how the word should be spelled: 'W-i-n, *win*, d-e-r, *der*, winder, a casement,' he said. His justification, if he had thought it necessary to have one, would doubtless have been that the word should be pronounced the way it was spelled, and spelled the way it was pronounced. In the same way today, thousands of teenagers know without thinking that the word *of* is usually pronounced *uv*—think of the phrases *Duke of Edinburgh* or *man of means*. So too is the word *have*, when it is shortened in spoken English: *I would've thought so*. So the interviewers who automatically bin job application forms on which are written sentences like *I would of thought* are making a big mistake. The applicants are not necessarily ignorant and illiterate: rather, admittedly in a slightly topsy-turvy way, they are following the ancient principle of the union between written and spoken English. Yeah, right.

More seriously, the uneasy relationship between speech and writing is responsible for many of the horrors that foreigners experience when they try to learn English. The best known is the infamous English *gh*, which may either be silent, as in *bright, fought* or *through*, or pronounced as an *f*, as in *cough, laugh* or *tough*—just imagine the fun a non-native speaker has with the word *Loughborough*. Four hundred years or so ago, the *gh* was generally pronounced at the back of the throat, in much the same way as a Scotsman might say *loch*, or a Welshman *Llanelli*. Over a period of about a century, this sound was gradually dropped from mainstream English, and replaced sometimes by silence and sometimes by *f*. The writing stayed the same, but the language had moved on.

That ancient *gh* sound did not vanish everywhere—it simply retreated north and west. Northern accents still retain it—think of *a braw, bricht, moonlicht nicht* in Scotland— and the effect of Celtic languages in Wales and Ireland kept it alive in place-names there. And

246

where it did disappear, it left its ghost behind. The *gh* had affected vowels which went before it in an apparently random way, lengthening some and rounding others, leaving us with the linguistic slough that is *cough*, *rough*, *bough* and *through*. Which is tough. Thoroughly tough.

The close link between English and French is another reason why English spelling is such a mess. Many of the French words that flooded across the Channel with the Norman invaders in 1066 have been so thoroughly assimilated by now that no one thinks of them as foreign— words like *army* (from *armée*), *judge* (from *juge*), *jury* (from *jurée*) and *prison* (from *prisoun*) may tell us something about the way the new regime sought to capture the hearts and minds of the Saxons, but they are all completely accepted today as English words with English pronunciations. It can take hundreds of years—the word *siege*, for example, imported into the language in the fourteenth century, has developed an English *ee* vowel instead of its French *ee-eh*, and also shifted the pronunciation of the final consonant from a French *zh* to a more English-sounding *dj* as in *hedge*. Other words which came more recently, such as *rouge* and *beige*, imported in the eighteenth and nineteenth centuries respectively, retain their French-sounding *zh*, though it too is clearly being replaced by a more Anglo-Saxon *dj*. They don't become English overnight.

But it's not simply a matter of longevity—*menu* arrived only in the early nineteenth century, and is now so thoroughly part of the language that it has developed its own momentum and extended its meaning into the world of computers. More to the point, it has also shifted its pronunciation, so that the original French *m'noo* has acquired an English *eh* in the middle to go with the yod—the *yoo* sound—at the end.

Despite the changes in spelling and punctuation which mean that we struggle to read anything written before the thirteenth or fourteenth centuries, and we would struggle even more to understand anyone speaking much before the sixteenth, the language we speak remains overwhelmingly based on Old English. Almost all the words we use most commonly—structural or form words such as *the, of, and* or *to*, and the names of everyday things like *man, friend, son, daughter, home*—come straight from the Anglo-Saxons. Even so, there have been so many French importations that there is a good case for describing modern English as a mixture of Anglo-Saxon and French—the writer Alexandre Dumas even described English, rather rudely, as nothing more than French pronounced badly. French clusters of letters like the *eau* of *beauty* no longer look strange, even though the pronunciation has changed over the centuries

248

from the French *oh* of the thirteenth century to the English *yew* of today.

That's not to say that the English have ever been at ease with French. 'Préparez-vous,' Winston Churchill warned a French audience after the war, in an accent that was so aggressively and uncompromisingly English it could have been dug up from an Anglo-Saxon burial mound. 'Je vais parler en français: une entreprise terrifiante, et qui sera une dure épreuve pour votre amitié envers la Grande-Bretagne.'—'I am going to speak in French: a terrifying enterprise, which will be a serious test for your friendship towards Great Britain.' The British have been testing French friendship by blundering like Anglo-Saxon bullocks through the delicate Limoges china-shop of their language for centuries.

There are differences of stress and intonation between the two languages, as well as different-sounding vowels and consonants, but one reason for the success of the Auld Alliance between Scotland and France—apart from a mutual dislike of the nation in between—might be the fact that Scots have an immediate advantage in trying to speak French because their vowel sounds are similar. Imagine a Scotsman asking for a bottle of merlot—his *mairloh* would be much closer to the French pronunciation than a buttoned-up English *murloh*. The French have never trusted what the English do to their language—they could never understand, for instance, why the British version of *The Magic Roundabout*, a children's cartoon of the 1960s, featured a dog, Dougal, which, they thought, was clearly named after their famous war-time leader, General De Gaulle. Was this some vile Anglo-Saxon slur on France's greatest war hero? And sometimes they get their own back: the great general's wife, Mme Yvonne De Gaulle, caused consternation at a British Embassy dinner party when the conversation turned to what the guests would most desire in life. 'A penis,' said this grandest of *grandes dames* with superb confidence. And, oblivious to the shocked silence, she repeated with panache, 'A penis. Personal 'appiness.'

*   *   *

When a French word is adopted into English, its pronunciation and spelling generally shift together, each one affecting the other: when the fashionable French idea of fastening up letters or parcels in little packages spread across the Channel early in the eighteenth century, the *beau-monde* referred to them as *envelopes* with a French pronunciation of *onv'llop*. It is unlikely that they would have attempted a French nasal *on*, so the pronunciation would have been very much an English version of the word from the start; and within a few years, people were lengthening the final syllable in the way that an *e* on the end of a word in English would lead them to expect. The word had become an awkward Anglo-French hybrid, with a French *on* at the front and an English *-ope* to end with, and so it remained for some hundred and fifty years. In the 1930s, the *Oxford English Dictionary* noted that the *on* pronunciation was still very frequently heard, although it noted rather sniffily that 'there is no good reason for giving a foreign sound to a word which no one regards as alien'. Today, that pronunciation is dying out—the *Longman Pronunciation Dictionary* of 1990 suggests that 78 per cent of people said *en*, compared with 22 per cent saying *on*. Most people under about 60 would talk about an *enn-vellope*, rather than an *onvelope*. The word's assimilation into English is more or less complete.

That's still happening with the word *genre*, which presents an English tongue with three pronunciation problems in quick succession— a French *zh*, followed by a nasal *on*, and then a final French *r*. The word was first used in English in the early nineteenth century, and pronounced as a French word for decades. Today, as it moves away from French and into English, it is increasingly heard with an anglicized *j* as in *judge*, a completely un-nasal *onn* in the middle, and a much breathier *-ruh* at the end—*jonn-ruh*. As the word becomes more familiar, so the pronunciation shifts to fit in with the habits of the English language rather than those of the French. Whether you want to call it the dumbing-down of the language or a natural process of assimilation is a matter of personal choice, but it's a fair bet that within the next few decades, *zhon-r* will have gone the way of *onv'llop*, and the only pronunciation to be heard will be *jonnruh*, with the unfamiliar *-ruh* the only clue to its foreign antecedents. There are a few other words, all originally from French, which end in *-re*—*centre*, *theatre* and *metre*, for instance—but there, the *r* is either silent, in British English, or after the *-uh* vowel in American. Perhaps, over time, the pronunciation of *genre* will change to *jennuh* in Britain, by analogy with the other *-re* words, and maybe the Americans will start to spell it *gener*.

Today, English speakers can cope with the unexpected vowels of *ensemble*, and even have a stab at one or both of the nasal sounds, unfamiliar as they are, but will frequently replace the delicate final French *l* with a rough Anglo-Saxon *-ull*, so that the word comes out *onsombull*, like another uneasy cross-Channel hybrid. Which is, in a sense, what it has become. *Ambience* retains its two nasal consonants for a few speakers—I remember a Soho bar-owner watching as an unsuccessful would-be customer bounced down the stairs after being thrown out. 'Get out!' he was shouting after him. 'You're ruining my bloody

252

ambience!' He was particular about the nasals—but more and more frequently, the word is turned into a more friendly, English *amm-bi-unce*. Other words, like *parachute*, fit so easily that their foreign origins are barely discernible—*parachute* loses its French *r*, of course, and swaps the *a* sound in the middle of the word for a generalized English *uh*, while still others retain lingering memories of their past. The French word *façade*, for instance, lost its unfamiliar cedilla under the *c* as soon as it crossed the Channel, and over its 300-year history as an English word has seen its second vowel change from a short French *a* to a more familiar *ah*—but, at least in Britain, it still has not acquired the common *ayd* sound, as in *made* or *fade*. The US, of course, is another matter—and, with *fassayd* rather than *fassahd* being heard increasingly frequently on this side of the Atlantic as well, it is probably only a matter of time before it completes its naturalization. The word *garage*, which made the crossing early in the twentieth century, is in a similar position. Like *façade*, it still—just— retains an *ah* vowel, but is increasingly being anglicized to *garridge*. There is also, incidentally, some uncertainty about the stress with which it is pronounced: while the French would say *garAGE*, English speakers are more or less evenly split over whether to put the stress on the first or second syllable. In fact, the *Longman Pronunciation Dictionary* lists five different pronunciations—*garARdge, gARRidge, GArrarzh, g'rARzh* and *g'rARdge*. With *GARRidge*, there is no argument over stress, and once it becomes the generally-accepted pronunciation, the word will have become completely assimilated into the language. [When it refers to music, it is invariably garridge. 'You'd get beaten up if you said garAGE,' my informant told me.]

We've already seen how a French menu can sort out the *moutons* from the *chèvres*—but the distinction starts before you even get in the door: the *LPD* gives no fewer than fifteen different acceptable ways of pronouncing the word *restaurant* in English. A large part of the problem, of course, concerns the final nasal syllable of the French word, on which a few people still insist. *Rest'ront* with a defiantly English final *t* is getting more common, but most people now settle for an intermediate *rest'ron*, with a simple *n* to replace the nasal sound. The word has been in the language for nearly 200 years, and it has gradually lost the guttural *r*'s, the entire *oh* syllable in the middle, and now the distinctive French ending which it originally boasted. Once upon a time, back in its days as an exclusively French expression, *restaurant* was simply the present participle of the verb *restaurer*, which means *to restore*—a place for *restoring* oneself with good food and drink. The changes in its pronunciation have probably been helped by the existence of a familiar English word, *rest*, which goes right back to an Anglo-Saxon original. Is it too middle-aged and grumpy to think it rather sad that a *rest'ron* should now simply be a place to slump back, *rest*, and shovel in burgers and chips? Far better, surely, to avoid the confusion, and rely on a good old English word like—er—*café*? Or *bistro*? Or *pizzeria*? Or *kebab-house*? Or perhaps a *rotisserie* or a *trattoria*?

And that, of course, is precisely the point. These words become English as the language changes. A few of the originally foreign sounds, like the *tz* in the middle of *pizzeria*, establish themselves in English, but generally English speakers adapt them to their own accent. They are as much a part of the language as roast beef—which was, of course, originally French anyway—it's just that *beef* has had several centuries longer to settle into the language. It's ironic that the French should refer to the English as *rosbifs*, thus taking a French word, *boeuf*, that has been given an English pronunciation, *beef*, and turning it back into a French pronunciation, *bif*. It's a perfect example of what goes around coming around.

These anglicizations may be bad French or Italian, but they are better English—and when people try too hard with foreign languages, they often get them wrong anyway. It may be only a minor error—many English people, for instance, insist on giving *Beijing* a French-sounding *zh* in the middle, presumably on the slightly shaky grounds that it sounds foreign, and that since *Beijing* is a foreign word, it must be right. The Chinese, who ought to know, insist that the word—which in fact is two words in their language (*Bei* means north and *Jing* capital)—has a *j* sound that is every bit as English as *jam* or *January*. A similar indignity is often inflicted on the French phrase *coup de grace* by people who, presumably with some vague memory that French final *s*'s tend to be silent, pronounce it *coo de gra*.

On the other hand, making too much effort can make you look decidedly foolish: generations of young men, anxious to impress their girlfriends with their command of French as well as with their knowledge of wine, may have been much too wise and well-informed to ask for *clarray*—but have then gone on to find Moët & Chandon on the wine list and confidently demanded a bottle of *Mway ay Chandon*. Among these pretentious young men might have been the scriptwriters for the BBC's *Only Fools and Horses*, who thought it was a good joke to show how stupid Del Boy was by making him pronounce the *t* in *Moët*. Oops! The problem is that although M. Claude Moët, the founder of the firm, was French, his name was Dutch, and so it should be pronounced *Mwett*. Since M. Moët died around 250 years ago, he's not likely to care, and, as long as people keep buying the champagne, neither are his descendants—but perhaps the story is a warning against trying to be too clever.

In the United States, spelling has always followed pronunciation more closely—think of *plow*, *catalog*, or *favorite*, for instance—which, by giving people a false sense of security, has led to worse experiences with foreign-looking words. A succession of American senators, congressmen, journalists and commentators has stepped up to wrestle with the name of Iraq's Abu Ghraib prison. *Aboogarrib, Abbergrayb, Boogrib*. Presumably frightened by the guttural Arabic *gh*, which comes from further back in the throat than any westerner ever goes except when he is trying to spit up something particularly unpleasant, they trample over the rest of the syllables in a panic. But traditionally, English speakers have taken a rather lordly view of the way the rest of the world speaks—the American author Mark Twain certainly had no time for foreign pronunciations. 'They spell it Vinci and pronounce it Vinchy; foreigners always spell better than they pronounce,' he said.[58] Lord Byron similarly left no doubt in his rhyming couplets of how he believed his hero Don Juan's name should be pronounced. He couldn't find any contemporary figures, he said, who were 'Fit for my poem (that is, my new one). So, as I said, I'll take my friend Don

Juan.'**59**

People who insist on twisting the rhyme and metre to indulge their pseudo-Spanish accents and call him Don *Huan* presumably also refer to Cervantes' famous knight as *Don Ki-hotay*. Which is, to say the least, quixotic, or rather, ki-hotic—and would, if they were going to be consistent, probably mean referring to the poet himself as *Thervantes*, with a properly Castilian lisp.

But just in case smug Britons enjoy laughing at the Americans' naïve mangling of *Leicester* or *Gloucester*, they should remember that they have their own problems once they cross the Atlantic. The Mojave Desert, of course, is tricky at first sight for anyone not familiar with Native American languages—although those who correct an ignorant foreigner talking about the *Moh-jayve* might usefully be reminded that the actual Native American word is *hàmakháav*, which is anyway barely within shouting distance of the modern 'correct' *Mohahvay*. And there are plenty of other linguistic traps waiting for the unwary traveller. One European visitor in Georgia in the Southern States, already wary because of stories of hillbillies scraping squashed animals off the road to put in their stew pot, was horrified to see the menu of an Atlanta pizza house reviewed in a local newspaper. 'The pizzas,' it read, 'are a mongrel mix of too much of a good thing—escargot, shrimp, smoked salmon, duck confit—and weirdness: quail eggs, caviar, mole . . .' 'Mole!' he shrieked in horror, childhood images of Moley, Ratty and the *Wind in the Willows* swimming before his eyes. It took several minutes for his amused hosts to reassure him that, far from serving little furry animals on its pizzas, the restaurant was simply offering its own version of a traditional Mexican chocolate-based sauce— *mohl-ay*, in short, rather than *mohl*. The French silent *t*'s of *escargot* and *confit* had presented him with no difficulty, but the unexpected *-ay* sound derived from the original Aztec word *molli* had caught him out. In its more familiar form of *guacamole* he might have recognized it—but even there, British diners seem to choose more or less at random between *gwakamohl*, *gwakamool*, *gwakamohl-ay* and *guakamool-ay*.

By contrast, no one in America, Britain, or the rest of the world would be confused by *pizza*, even though the word and its *tz* middle consonant are just as foreign to English. The degree to which it has been assimilated into the language by frequent use can be measured by the fact that people invariably talk about *pizzas* with an English *s* plural, rather than the more 'correct' Italian *pizze*, which was used when the word first appeared in English in the mid-1930s. In fact, the *tz*-sounding double-*z* was already known in English from the use of Italian terms like *pizzicato*, which was in use in the nineteenth century, and *piazza*, first seen in the sixteenth, so there was never any serious confusion, even though the traditional English z sound of words like *buzzard* or *mizzen* goes back for hundreds of years. *Pizza* took the new *tz* out of the orchestra pit and the travelogue, and into everybody's daily life. It still remains tied to words that have a clear Italian origin, so that even relatively new words like *pizzazz* retain the traditional English sound. Even the Italian restaurant chain Zizzi pronounces itself *zeezee*, rather than *zitzi*—possibly so that it doesn't remind its customers of zits, spots and teenage acne. And of course, there's *mezzanine*—undoubtedly Italian, and yet sometimes pronounced *metz* and sometimes *mezz*.

Often, the spelling can follow the pronunciation to make a new English word from the original foreign one—and not just with French or Italian, of course. In the seventeenth century, the explorer Captain John Smith, of Pocahontas fame, tried to reproduce the Spanish word *cacarucha* in English. His version, *cacarootch*, simply removed the Spanish word-ending, but within another thirty years or so, people were writing, and presumably speaking, of *cockroches*, which rapidly metamorphosed into the modern *cockroaches*. Cocks were familiar enough, and roaches were already well known in English as a small fish, so the name stuck—nothing to do with either cocks or roaches, but simply one that sounded right in English. It was not for another 200 years that *cockroach* was shortened to *roach* in the United States, allegedly by prim young East Coast girls who didn't want to sully their mouths with anything as crude as *cock*. In the less fastidious—or less imaginative—Britain, such a thought never occurred to them.

The same sort of process, with a little more imagination thrown into the mix, accounts for the John Dory, the tasty little fish known to biologists as *Zeus faber*. The *Dory* part is a simple anglicization of the French word *doré*, which means golden, while the *John*, according to some dictionaries, is a similar adaptation of *jaune*, the French for yellow. It's an attractive idea—*jaune doré* transformed into a no-nonsense name that sounds almost as English as John Bull—but the only catch is that nobody has been able to find the French phrase *jaune doré* attached to the fish. It seems more likely, if less satisfying, that someone attached the *John* as a bit of a joke in the eighteenth century. (This, at any rate, is the view of the *Oxford English Dictionary*. The fish had been known as a *dory* since the fifteenth century, and John Dory was the hero of a popular seventeenth-century ballad.) But whatever the truth of that, it is still a name that exists solely because of its sound, and not because of any meaning it might have.

European languages are not usually a serious problem for English speakers—they are, after all, part of the same family—and even words from further afield can often be gently shoehorned into English pronunciations that leave them more or less recognizable. The Japanese *judo* and *karate*, brought into the country in the nineteenth and twentieth centuries respectively, have been assimilated easily enough. The Japanese pronunciations *juudor* and *karatEH* slip into English with only a couple of slight adjustments, and their clearly foreign appearance fits with the fact that they denote explicitly foreign skills. The same applies to names like *kangaroo*, said to be from a local aborigine word *gang-oo-roo*; or to *chimpanzee*, from a Bantu language of Angola, or to *jaguar*, which came via the Portuguese from a South American Tupi word which referred to any large meat-eating animal. The *aroo*, *anzee* and *guar* are all foreign to English (yes, I know about *guardian* and *guarantee*, but since the *u* there is silent, and simply hardens the *g*, it seems to make the point), but all the individual sounds are easy to pronounce, so the words have survived. The *giraffe* gets its name originally from the Arabian *ziraffa*, the letters *z, s* and *j* being almost interchangeable when Europeans wrote down Arabic words in the sixteenth century. But when words come from languages that have completely different sound-systems, then assimilating them into English is more difficult.

When the English first wanted to write about a new antelope that had been discovered in southern Africa in the early nineteenth century, they used either the Dutch term of the explorers who had first found the creature—*wildebeest*—or the explorers' version of the original Bushmen's word, *gnu*. *Wildebeest* was easy enough to pronounce, although the Dutch *v* for *w* was unfamiliar, but *gnu* was a brave stab by the Dutch at an impossibility. The Bushmen's language included several different types of click, and their word *gnu* began with one and ended with another, so the initial *g* of the English version was originally an attempt to reproduce at least one of these clicks. When the word first appeared in English, the *g* was pronounced, but it was lost very quickly by analogy with other English words such as *gnaw* or *gnat*. The Anglo-Saxon words had taken several centuries to lose their initial *g*-sound, but the poor old gnu lost it within a few decades. It was probably the Flanders and Swann song of the early 1960s that saw the *g* off—*I'm a gnu, I'm a gnu, The g-nicest work of g-nature in the zoo.*

The song made the original pronunciation, *g-noo*, comic—and nobody likes to sound silly.

It's not only the vowels and consonants that change when a word is taken up by another language. As we saw with Indian English, it can be much harder for a foreign speaker to capture the different rhythms and stress of an unfamiliar language—the English pronunciation of *Paris*, for instance, not only sounds the final *s* which the French leave silent, it also reverses the stress pattern. Where the French say *parEE*, the English say *PARiss*. It's hard to see why, other than a natural British desire to wind up the French. A lot of our place-names have their stress on the first syllable—*London, Oxford, Brighton, Scotland, Cornwall*—but we seem to manage a second-syllable stress quite happily with *Berlin*, *Madrid* and even *Marseilles*. Perhaps it is easier to see how the change of stress works with non-English speakers talking English— Palestinian politicians, for example, talking about their homeland. The Arabic word for Palestine is *filistEEN*—like the Philistines in the Bible, but with the stress on the final syllable. Many Arabs who speak English have an almost perfect command of vowel sounds and consonants, but still speak with the stresses and intonation of the language they know best. However good their English, most Arabs will talk about *PalestINE*, and never *PALestine*: they can change the vowel sounds to match the new language, but the stresses remain the same.

Finally, it's as well to remember that spoken language can play tricks. Words can have a separate existence from their meaning: the sounds that signify one thing in one language or at one time can have quite another meaning in another. Names, in particular, of people or of places, can start with one meaning and end up with quite another. When Mr and Mrs Kwok named their son, they had no idea that one day he would be living in the United States and might regret their choice. Back in China, they had seen nothing untoward about the name Fuk King Kwok—but after a brief discussion with the Illinois driving-licence office shortly after moving to the States, young Mr Kwok changed his name to Andy for a quiet life in his new home.

A town in western Austria has suffered for years because for some reason English-speaking tourists keep stealing its road-sign. Its name, which means 'the people of Focko', and has a long and honourable history going back at least a thousand years, is *Fucking*. In fact, if they don't like people laughing at their name, they don't exactly help themselves. At one time, the sign had beneath it one of those notices familiar from similar towns on main roads in Britain and all over the world, asking passing motorists not to break the speed limit and endanger the town's children. Under the town's name was a picture of two children, and the ambiguous warning 'Bitte, nicht so schnell'—'Not so fast, please'! In France in the early 1950s, the French drinks company

Perrier thought it had simply captured the sound of a fizzy drink when it called its new lemonade *Pschitt*. Generations of delighted British schoolboys on holiday have interpreted it differently. And then, of course, there are the Austrian mountain *Wank*, the street in the German town of Johanneskirchen called *Furkhoffstrasse*, and the two villages, one in Orkney and one in Shetland, which rejoice in the name of *Twatt*. We all know someone who ought to live there. But it's fair to assume that those who named these places would have been blissfully unaware of the vulgar meanings their chosen names would eventually acquire in English—as, no doubt, would have been the founding fathers of *Arsoli* in Italy, *Bollock* in the Philippines, *Crap* in Albania, and *Wangqing* in China. The list is virtually endless.

And it can be true of English names, too— French ski-instructors (many of them, anyway) will go to any lengths not to have to call down the mountain to any of their English pupils who happen to be called Penny. It's a charming name in English, but has a slightly different ring in French. After all, how would *you* like to walk up and down a mountain slope shouting 'Penis'? In fact, the French are extremely sensitive about these things: French teachers have a guilty secret which they have kept from their more inquisitive pupils for years. In the sentence *Ce que l'on dit*, the word *ce* means *that, que* means *which, on* means *one*,

266

and *dit* means *says: That which one says.* 'So what,' a bright pupil might ask, 'does the word *l'*, before *on*, mean?' The honest answer is nothing at all: the *l'* is a meaningless flap of the tongue. Every French teacher in Britain that I have ever spoken to—except one—has hedged nervously around the reason for its existence, a bit like parents telling their young children how babies are found under gooseberry bushes. The fact is that *l'* serves the same purpose as those other meaningless little flaps, which the Victorians allegedly used to protect themselves from the crushing sexual humiliation of having to look at their table-legs. Without its protection, *que* and *on* would become *qu'on.* Instead of *That which one says*, the sentence would mean *That 'con' says*—and *that* would shake the Academie Française to its very foundations, because *con* means—oh come on, work with me. How many one-syllable expletives beginning with the letter *c* can you think of?

But all these words, French and English, must have seemed appropriate, serviceable and even unremarkable at one time. In their own languages, the various names probably still do. The point about all of them is that you can never predict what geography, history and the evil genius of language are going to do to your bright ideas.

267

CHAPTER NINE

Today and Tomorrow
Estuary English and how the language is changing now

You don't have to be alive very long to realize that practically nothing ever turns out as it was intended—and few things are as unpredictable as language. For the last five centuries or more, the economic and political power of the capital city has meant that the language of London, first written and then spoken, was presented as the standard to which cultured people should aspire: the early nineteenth-century writer Benjamin Humphrey Smart, in his *Grammar of English Sounds* in 1812, was quite definite on the subject. 'The imitation of a Londoner or a person who pronounces like one is the only method by which a just utterance can be acquired,' he declared.

He was, of course, speaking about the wealthy and fashionable people who gathered around the Court, not about the poor who made up the vast majority of the population of the city. No one, it seems, likes urban voices. Smart, when he writes about them, seems to be holding his nose so tightly that the words will hardly come out: 'There are two pronunciations even in London: that of the

268

well-bred and that of the vulgar. The well-bred speaker employs a definite number of sounds, which he utters with precision, distinctness, and in their proper places; the vulgar speaker misapplies the sounds, mars, or alters them.' Some of his complaints sound quaint today— he was offended, for instance, by the 'corruption' of the *e* in *perpetrate*, so it came out as *perputtrate*, and by the failure to sound the vowels in *mercy* and *virtue* properly, so they were pronounced *mursy* and *vurtue*, rather than *mairsy* and *veertue*—but others, such as the *oo* sound replacing *yoo* in *duty* or *Tuesday*, or the pronunciation of *boil* as *bile*, are more familiar. The sound of Cockney, it is fairly safe to say, was not music in his ears.

What a delicious irony it is, then, that the London speech which seems to be most influential in our own day should be not the precision and distinctness of the well-bred which Sharp praised, but the vulgar corruption which he despised. Cockney, it seems, has transformed itself into Mockney, Jockney and any other -ockney that an idle headline-writer can devise, as it sets about taking over the world. As Estuary English, the slightly more restrained name it was given in the 1980s,[60] this modern version of London speech is the pantomime villain for parents who are desperate for their children to speak 'properly' and for earnest defenders of regional accents alike. The *glo'all* stop, it seems, is spreading

269

like a virus.

That, at least, is the journalists' view, repeated in a whole series of articles over the last few years warning that we are headed for a world in which we all talk like the cast of *EastEnders*, and probably eat jellied eels down the Old Bull and Bush as well, while singing 'Knees Up Muvver Brahn'. In the early 1990s, the distinguished linguistic scholar Paul Coggle predicted: 'Before long we may find that the users of glottal stops have not only become the majority, but have also assumed powerful positions in the land'[61]—and sure enough, in 1997, Britain found itself with a prime minister who casually leaned back on television sofas and stopped his glottis like mad as he crafted the image of a straight-talking man of the people. Just a few months after the election, he told the cameras that he had been 'hur' and 'upse'' by criticism of his role in Labour's decision to accept a huge donation from the Formula One millionaire Bernie Ecclestone. He was, he said, 'a pre'y straigh' guy.'

Apart from politicians with a point to prove, it's particularly popular among pop stars and teenagers: *Jewonn'a cumm'a my pah'y?* was the way one writer chose to demonstrate it.[62] But like most things, it's more complicated than the newspapers suggest. The accepted theory is that pronunciations such as *bo'ull* for bottle, *li'ull* for little, and *Ga'wick* for *Gatwick*, have

270

spread insidiously across England from their origins in working-class Cockney, infecting much of the country's youth on the way. That's probably more or less how this particular habit of speech did spread—but it's worth pointing out in passing that the infection, if that's what it is, is far more widespread and longer-lived than most people suppose. As we have seen, there is much more to the letter *t* than the carefully-tapped *tuh*, and elderly gentlemen who would rather die of thirst than ask for a *bo'ull of wa'er* will habitually stop the final *t* on words like *right*, particularly when they come in the middle of sentences, and before another consonant. *I'm righ' behind you* is much easier to say than *I'm right behind you*. The northern contraction of *the, t'*, as in *trouble at t'mill*, is little more than a slightly more vocalized glottal stop—and there are few things less like a Cockney than a Yorkshireman.

More than twenty years after the phrase was coined, linguists still argue about how directly Estuary English derives from Cockney. Certainly, several of its features have always been common in other parts of the country. The Blairish glottal stop that causes such annoyance, for instance, is common not just in London speech, but in Geordie and Glaswegian as well. The Yorkshire *t'* is another example that has existed for centuries. It's easier to do than to describe—closing off the larynx briefly and then allowing a pulse of air

271

out in an explosive burst, almost like the beginning of a cough. Despite the fact that the most common criticism aimed at it is that it is an example of 'lazy speech', it sounds like a pretty tricky operation—but even so, it's common in many other languages. The Arabic phrase, *allahu akbar* (*God is almighty*), for instance, starts with a glottal stop, and it's also frequently used in Hebrew, German and French, and in other languages from North America to the Polynesian islands.

In English, too, glottal stops have always been much more common than the criticism would make you think, although since they are not part of the Australian accent, it's probably only in the last 200 years or so, since the first settlers sailed to Australia, that they have become widely used. The letter *t* seems to be fairly fragile in any case: the classic tapped *tuh* sound that we would instinctively say that it represented has always been only one of a number of ways it is pronounced. Try tapping a *t* in the middle of *bottle*, for instance, and you end up sounding like a 3-year-old child. Elsewhere, as in *picture* or *lecture*, it comes out more like a *ch*—*pict-yure* or *lect-yure* would be almost impossibly prissy, and there would be very few people who would ever have described the 1950s musical as *Annie, Get Your Gun*. Betchya.

For at least two and a half centuries, the *t*'s have been regularly dropped from words like *listen*, *castle* and *jostle*. Even the existence of *haste*, *wrest* and *soft* couldn't save them in *hasten*, *wrestle*, and *soften*. *Often*, on the other hand, seems to be an odd case. Early in the twentieth century, most people pronounced the *t*, until *of'en* began to take over. Now *often* with a *t* seems to be making a comeback, particularly among young people. It infuriates them when you point it out.

In the early 1900s, the silent assault on *t*'s before other consonants began to spread: first, even self-consciously 'correct' speakers began to downgrade them in their informal moments, so that phrases like *Quite nice* and *night duty* became *Qui' nice* and *nigh' duty*. The habit was virtually unstoppable: in the late 1960s, BBC announcers referred to the television snooker programme as *Po' Black*, and nobody even noticed. Today, the charmingly-named chain of clothes stores is universally known as *Fa' Face*, I don't believe I have ever heard anyone say *seat-belt* rather than *sea'belt*, and planes that don't land at Heathrow have for years had the option of flying into *Ga'wick*. Then glottal stops replacing *t*'s at the end of words like *hat*, *can't*, or *split* became commonplace, so that today, even though a sentence like *I can' fin' my ha'* looks odd on the printed page, it probably represents the way most of us would say it. Especially if we needed our hat in a hurry.

Elsewhere, though, the habit causes more

problems. A glottalized *t* between two vowels, as in *bo'll o' bi'er* for *bottle of bitter*—or *glo'all (glottal)* itself, come to that—has been variously described as the social equivalent of a tattoo, sporting a stud in your tongue, or wearing a baseball cap back to front. Either way, it's not good news. It's the vowels on each side that make the difference: you can ask for your beer in a *pin' glass* in the smartest bar, but if you asked for *a pin' of bi'er*, you might sound out of place. If you think of Estuary English, like any other accent, as a spectrum, which ranges from the restrained and upper-crust version spoken by Tony Blair through to the broad Cockney of some of the characters in *EastEnders*, this aspect of it falls very definitely at the Cockney end: Prince William, interviewed by the BBC as he left St Andrews University, declared that 'It's very important to see wha' you wan'a do and go for i'"—but when it came to 'getting through the next few months,' and not being 'wrapped up in cotton wool,' his *t*'s were tapped like tacks. Both Prince William and Tony Blair, alongside the features of Estuary English that attract such comment, also have other aspects of their accents that come straight from their public school, university backgrounds: Tony Blair's *u*'s, for instance, are so unrounded that they sound almost like *e*'s, so that *results* comes out as *reselts*, and *culminating* as *kelminating*, while the word *ensure* comes out as *in-shoo-er*—pure

274

Edinburgh. The young prince meanwhile tells his interviewer that *life up he-ah* at St Andrews has been *ve'y good fun*.

The glottal *t*, and especially the glottal *t* between two vowels, is the habit that most people fix on when they talk about Estuary English—but it is only one of several hallmarks of the accent. Another particularly noticeable one is the replacement of the letter *l* either at the end of a word or before another consonant by a short *uh* sound, so that *hill* becomes *hi-uw*, or *milk* becomes *mi-uwk*. John Major and Norman Tebbit, both of them with London backgrounds, are just two well-known politicians who use this pronunciation, although again, they are clearly at the opposite end of the language spectrum from the archetypal Cockney barrow-boy. Hearing Sir Alan Sugar stressing the importance of 'Sows, sows, sows,' on *The Apprentice* on the BBC, it takes a moment to realize that he is not suggesting that the ambitious would-be apprentices sitting before him look like pigs, but lecturing them about what they should be concentrating on as businessmen and women. 'Sales, sales, sales,' is his message. Jonathan Ross, too, emphasizes his London *l*'s: 'We have free hours to fiw, and we're going to fiw it in the only way we know hee-ow,' he either warns or promises, depending on your point of view, at the start of his Radio Two show— demonstrating at the same time two other traditional London features. The *th* sound becomes *f*, which is simple enough, but the vowel sounds push each other out of the way like an old-fashioned London bus queue. A short *o* becomes *or*, *oh* becomes *ow*, and *ow* is lengthened to *ee-ow*, so that *cough* becomes *cawff*, *no* becomes *now*, and *now* becomes *nee-ow*. The vowel in a word like *caught* becomes much tighter and more rounded—but again, it's important to remember the spectrum. All these vowel changes are less marked the further the speaker gets from a broad London accent.

There are many aspects of Cockney that are not reflected at all in Estuary English. The pronunciation of *a* as *eye*, which makes *paint* sound almost the same as *pint*, and which leads to the old joke about the difference between a buffalo and a bison—you can't pee in a buffalo—is still definitely a working-class habit. So, of course, is *h*-dropping, in London as in most of the rest of England: *Harold Hill* becomes *'Arold 'Ill* and *Hackney* sounds like a skin complaint, but it's still not a habit that's been picked up in Estuary English. Tony Blair is no more likely to talk about *New Liebour* than Prince William is to refer to *me an' 'Arry*.

Those are examples from the Cockney end of the spectrum; somewhere in the middle comes Jonathan Ross's *fink* or the *vv* of *Big Bruvver*. Tony Blair and Prince William might not talk about *Fursday* or *Lady Fatcher*, for instance, but it is a pronunciation that would be heard quite frequently on television or in the street. Perhaps the *f* and *v* sounds are easier to produce—it's significant that small children often have trouble with their *th*'s—but it's not simply 'careless speech'. In fact, suggesting that it is might be an example of careless thought—because the distinction between the voiced *th* of *brother* and its unvoiced equivalent in *think* is retained just as carefully in the Cockney version. Where the *th* sound is voiced, as in *rather*, *another* or *brother*, it comes out as a *v*, and where it is unvoiced, as in *Matthew*, *Thursday* or *think*, as an *f*. No one—at least no native speaker of English—says *Big Bruffer* or *I don't vink so*: the sounds have changed but the distinction between voiced and unvoiced is observed as rigorously between *f* and *v* as it is between the sounds of *thin* and *them*.

None of these distinctions matter for the critics of Estuary English. The attacks on the way people speak are so bitter and vitriolic that there is clearly something else going on in the background. 'Lazy speaking', 'horrifying', and 'slovenly' are some of the milder criticisms. The journalist Michael Henderson, as we've seen, got hot under the collar over 'that ghastly Estuary sludge'; others have described it as 'London, of course, but debased London: slack-jawed, somnambulant London,' or—most grotesquely of all—

277

'Slobspeak, limp and flaccid—the mouths uttering it deserve to be stuffed with broken glass.' The only sane answer to rants like that is simply, 'Get a life!'—or rather, 'Ge' a life!'

The question which most of them come down to in the end is simply, 'Isn't it dreadful?' Pained as it sounds, it can really only be answered yes or no, which doesn't take us very far. What is much more interesting is to ask what is actually happening, and why it arouses such uncontrollable anger. Of course there are language changes going on, as they always have. In the past, they've often started in London where there was both the biggest mix of accents and also the most fashionable and influential society. But even so, many of them, such as the rounded *a* in *path*, *grass* and *castle* or the unrounded *u* in *cup* or *butter*, spread only as far as the Midlands, so that the line from the Severn to the Wash represents a sort of blurred and indistinct boundary between two different ways of speaking English. Those who like to see the workings of history played out in the modern world might like to note that—in very rough terms—that line seems to follow the boundary between the Anglo-Saxon kingdoms of Northumbria and Mercia some 1,300 years ago.

It is a frontier that is still more or less holding out today. There are changes in other big cities that seem almost to echo some of those spreading out from London, but to a great extent, it seems that Estuary English has reached no further than what might be called the '*bath*/*barth* boundary'. North of that fuzzy line, for all the scare stories about an irresistible take-over of the country, Estuary English has much less influence on general pronunciation than the traditional regional dialects that have been spoken for generations. Even in the big cities, where Liverpudlians saying *fink* and *bruvver* instead of *t'ink* and *brudder*, or Glaswegians talking about their *teef* (both examples taken from linguistic surveys) might seem to be part of a tide of Estuary English which is sweeping the nation, the situation is more complex than it seems. A more popular theory is that there is a new trend towards regionally-similar accents based on big centres of population. London speech is having an effect, but around Liverpool, Glasgow, Newcastle in the north-east, Birmingham in the West Midlands, and the Leeds-Bradford conurbation in West Yorkshire, there are homogenized regional accents developing. The local differences that used to exist between towns within the same region—between Sheffield and Barnsley, for instance—are rapidly being ironed out.

The reason isn't hard to find: as people around the cities travel more freely, whether commuting to work or visiting friends, shopping, watching football or going to the theatre, so their day-to-day contacts with people throughout the immediate region increase. For all Lord Reith's concern in the 1920s about the awesome responsibility of the BBC, it's face-to-face conversation that has the greatest influence on pronunciation, rather than television, radio, or films—after all, Scots who hear English accents every day on their televisions still speak like Scots; an Indian who lives in New Delhi and learns his English from the BBC's World Service will still speak it with an Indian accent rather than a BBC one.

Language changes so slowly that it's almost impossible to track the innovations and shifts as they happen—a bit like watching a tree come into leaf. Odd words like *skedule* for *shedule* may sound unfamiliar, or a particular habit like a glottal stop may start to attract attention, but the wider trends in the way people speak can often only be identified after they have happened. Who notices a butterfly flapping its wings? But to a certain extent, the anguished protests about Estuary English seem to be justified: English is changing, just not in the way they are suggesting. There is no simple Cockney take-over, but all the big cities, London included, are having an increasing influence on the way English is spoken in different parts of the country.

Put that way, it's no surprise: the way people spoke in a slow-moving rural society a hundred years ago is hardly likely to survive in a faster-paced urban world. But it's not the mere fact of change that arouses such bitterness. Everybody speaks differently at different times. What makes it harder for some people to accept Estuary English is that many of the supposedly 'new' pronunciations mirror the way they already speak themselves in their more relaxed moments: as we've seen, for example, the infamous glottal-stopped *t* is already fairly common in everyday, casual speech all over the country and across the various social classes. That provides the first clue to what is really going on.

People may change their style deliberately, to get across changes in meaning. Of course, stressing individual words can make an obvious difference, so that in the example earlier in the chapter, '*I* can't find my hat!' would suggest that somebody else might be able to; 'I *can't* find my hat!' would reject the suggestion that I could if I really put my mind to it, and 'I can't find my *hat*!' might mean that I could find pretty well anything else I wanted to look for, but not my hat. So much is pretty simple—but a change in style can be much more subtle. With the *t*'s tapped and the *d* perfectly enunciated, the sentence becomes a patient, almost challenging reminder of something you should have known all along—you could mentally almost add the phrase 'Dammit!' It's only when the sentence is a casual, neutral statement of fact that the *t*'s and the *d* start to vanish.

And that is the big change that is happening, not just in Britain, but throughout the industrialized world—society is getting much more casual. Many people bitterly resent it—but where once people would have behaved and spoken formally, now they are more relaxed. Politicians address the nation from the squashy sofas of breakfast television, rather than from behind polished wooden desks the size of football fields; schoolteachers in gowns are about as common as men in spats; the chancellor of the exchequer dines at the Mansion House in a lounge suit, when everyone else is in tails; and senior Conservative politicians leave their ties in their pockets. In every way, it is a less deferential world: in the early 1950s, the then Leader of the Opposition, Clement Attlee, was stopped by an importunate reporter as he returned from a foreign trip. The exchange that followed was a classic of broadcasting: 'Excuse me, sir, is there anything you would like to say to the nation?'—'No,' said Attlee, and off he went. Politicians would never expect to get away with that sort of high-handedness today—and in the same way, they adopt a much more easy-going and friendly style of speaking when they are being interviewed.

In a slightly less tight-lipped frame of mind, Attlee welcomed the United Nations to its first General Assembly in London in 1946. His tone of voice was not just upper-crust and irreproachably RP—after all, his background, like Tony Blair's, was public school, Oxford and the Bar—but it was also oratorical and mannered. 'Should there be a third world war—the long upward progress towards civilization—may be halted for generations—and the work of myriads—of men and women—through the centuries—be brought to nought,' he said. What sounds odd today is not just the grandiose phraseology—the 'long upward progress towards civilization' and the 'myriads of men and women'—but also the precise, clipped accents with which he talks about the *assembleh* and the *delegayts*, with the stress on the final syllable. He speaks, too, in grandiose, oratorical periods—the long gaps between his phrases are those of a man who is used to being listened to.

Politicians today, even in a comparably formal setting, are much more relaxed in their delivery. It's not only about pronunciation, but about style as well: in a keynote speech early in his leadership of the Conservative Party, David Cameron told the Foreign Policy Centre in London, 'Two principles lie behind much of what you do. That Britain has an important role to play in international affairs. And that foreign and domestic policy are deeply inter-connected. You're right about both.' His message was as serious as Attlee's sixty years earlier, but the style—short, terse phrases and informal expressions—is very different.

When the style is so relaxed, it's no surprise that the pronunciation should be relaxed as well—and of course the politicians, as they always do, are simply trying to mirror the way the wider world has changed. In the early days of broadcasting, a radio studio was an awe-inspiring place. Broadcasters sounded serious for just the same reason that people in early photographs looked so unsmiling: the technology was slightly threatening and not to be laughed at. Even in the 1970s, broadcasting was a different and more solemn business. Sue MacGregor, the former presenter of the BBC's *Today* programme on Radio 4, says that when she hears tapes of herself broadcasting thirty-five years ago, she is struck by how carefully enunciated and precise her voice sounds. 'I worked in South Africa in the 1960s, and everybody in broadcasting there spoke with a Southern British Received Pronunciation accent. They deliberately employed people who didn't sound South African,' she says. 'When I came to London, it was also true that there was a definite BBC voice—much more RP than the vast majority of people sound now.'

Men once had hats to raise, but when is the last time you saw someone raise his baseball cap to a lady? Whether that's a good thing or a bad thing is an argument that can go on for ever without being settled: the point is that it's happening. How you see it depends on where

284

you are standing—or, frequently, which sofa you are slouched on. It's not only Tony Blair's glottal stops that annoy people—his frequent casual *y'know*'s are just as much a feature of his laid-back interview style as his Estuary *t*'s. Shop assistants, too, are much more relaxed than they once were—there is, after all, no *t* to be swallowed or glottalized when you are called 'sir', but it's all too obvious when you've just been addressed as 'mate'. Or rather, 'may'. But friendliness can be misread as disrespect—so part of the problem is that people see a more easy-going style of speech as part of a breakdown in the order of society. Changes in the way people speak are obvious and easy to describe, at least on a superficial level, so they become a symbol of the unsettling changes in society as a whole. It's the glottal stop that gets it.

*   *   *

There are other changes going on too. In fact, once you get past fifty, it's probably impossible to resist the temptation to believe that language, like everything else, gets worse all the time. Nothing is ever as good as it was. Oddly, people have been complaining about that for at least 250 years. No less a figure than the High Master of St Paul's School, Alexander Gill, noted bitterly in the seventeenth century that the parents of some of his pupils insisted on saying *leave* instead of *lave* and *skoller* instead of *skollar*. He had a whole list of other complaints about sloppy speech, and since he was known to reinforce his opinions with the liberal application of the birch, it was probably as well to listen to him, even though it seems unlikely that anybody in the entire world spoke as he believed they should.

There were probably grumpy old men before him, too, complaining that nobody spoke as clearly as they used to. After all, people have always had a tendency to get slightly deaf as they get older, and to get slightly cross if they are reminded of it. It's also true that speech was probably always more musical and more beautifully pronounced in our youth, just as the songs were always better and the skies bluer. It's the same with soccer, sex and summers: the older we get, the better it was.

In fact, there is no objective evidence that speech is any less distinct and easy to understand today than it was three or four hundred years ago—but that is certainly not the same thing as saying that there have been no changes. All the processes of merging and splitting of sounds, the loss of syllables, and the lengthening and shortening of various vowels continue today just as they always have. Yesterday's 'sloppy speech' can become today's Received Pronunciation. In the 1930s, for instance, one of the BBC's senior linguistic advisers reported that there were many complaints about a growing tendency among announcers to shorten the long vowel before the *f* sound in words like *cough* and *off*. Instead of saying *cawff* and *awff*, as they were supposed to, the announcers were saying *coff* and *off*—in just the same way that the vast majority of people do today.[63] Seventy years on, *cawff* and *awff* would now be either almost impossibly old-fashioned or broad Cockney. And that trend is continuing: the short vowel is spreading to words such as *caught* and *ought*, where the spelling seems to suggest that *aw* might be more appropriate. *Caught* and *cot* don't sound the same—but they are often a lot closer than they used to be. Whether it's a good thing or bad is irrelevant: it's certainly not a change that makes speech any less easy to understand. That change, at least, is virtually complete.

So too is the merger between the vowels in the words *paw* and *pour*. Only a few decades ago, the second one would generally have been pronounced with a clear *or-uh* sound, but now there is practically no distinction between the two words. A similar thing is happening to the vowel in words like *fair*, where the vowel would have been closer to *ay-uh*, instead of the single *air* which is more common now. And in the word *our*, which used to be a clear *ow-er*—as it still is in much of the north of England—the vowel has opened out until the word often sounds very similar to *ah*. Only a few years ago, the recent Bisto advertisement on television—'Our time. Our family time. Ah, Bisto!' would not have been possible. It's hard to see how the world coped without such a literary gem.

One change which has caused problems for several decades is the mysterious Case of the Vanishing Yod. We are told that in the Hebrew alphabet, yod represents the contraction of the Infinite into the finite point of potentiality— but in the almost equally arcane world of academic linguistics, it has a role which is only slightly less controversial.**64**

The Hebrew letter yod happens to have the sound *y*, and so it is used in linguistics to represent the beginning of the vowel sound *oo* when words like *few* or *cute* are pronounced in British English. Those words are simple enough: the trouble comes because the yod used to be present in a whole range of different words, and it has gradually vanished—or rather, it is gradually vanishing. The writers of letters to the papers are frequently wrong when they blame the Americans for everything they think is at fault with the language, but this change, even though, as we've seen, it's always been particularly evident in East Anglia, may indeed be due to American influence. Yods, like proper cups of tea and unpasteurized cheese,

are much rarer in the US than in England—
the Americans, like the British, would have
fyoo, *cyoot* and *hyoomerus* for *few, cute* and
humorous, but words like *tune, dune* and *new*
would generally be pronounced *toon, doon* and
noo, while in most of Britain—except, for
some reason, in East Anglia—they would
usually be *tyoon, dyoon* and *nyew*.

Right? Wrong? Sloppy English? It depends
not just on who you ask (or whom you ask) but
on when you ask them. The world is changing,
and a fair rule of thumb is that the more
dogmatic you are, the more foolish you will
end up looking.

These changes happen insidiously, affecting
first one word and then another. With *culture*
and *soldier*, for instance, the transformation is
now generally accepted—but with *tune* and
endure, it is still gradually taking place. *T-yune*
and *end-yure* are still quite commonly heard,
but so are *choon* and *en-jure*. It is happening
literally as we speak.

Many changes are so small that they are
hardly noticed. When I was a child, I was
occasionally sent to the corner shop
(remember those?) to buy a packet of Quality
Street chocolates and toffees. Everyone, in
those days, would have talked about a *pakkit of
Kwolitti Street*—but now the second vowel of
both *packet* and *quality* would very probably
have changed to an *uh*. A *pakkut* of *Kwolutty
Street*. And it's changing further—the final *i* at

289

the end of *Quality* is likely now to have lengthened and tightened—imagine the word *settee* without the stress on the final syllable and you will get the idea; and of course, the final *t* of *Street* is an endangered species. It is many years since the second syllable of *orange* was pronounced as an *a*, if indeed it ever was. It used to be *i*, but like *packet* and *quality*, it has changed over the last few years to an *uh*. The same thing is happening to *eleven*: instead of *ileven*, it is increasingly pronounced as *uhleven*.

Small, unnoticeable changes like this gradually transform the way we speak. While the *i*'s in medicine have withered away from *meddyssin* to *met's'n*, *hooligan* and *officer*, by contrast, still generally keep them as a very brief and unstressed syllable. In *criminal* and *discipline*, the syllable remains, but it is often downgraded to an *uh* sound—the schwa that we met in an earlier chapter.

It all happens gradually, in incremental steps. A child, for example, might have heard the word *medicine* pronounced *meduhssin*, with the middle syllable downgraded to a schwa. To an adult who was used to talking about *medissin*, this would have sounded like an unusual but just about acceptable pronunciation, but to the child, it might have sounded like the normal way of saying the word. Years later, when the child heard someone pronounce the word *med'sin*, that would have seemed in turn like an unusual but just about acceptable pronunciation. And so, over a lengthy period, the word would change from *medissin* to *met's'n* in a series of steps which might each have seemed odd but hardly revolutionary to succeeding generations of adult speakers.

One survey took a selection of words where there is disagreement about pronunciation, and analysed the results according to age.[65] The vanishing yod that we saw earlier was a clear example of a change that is being made by young speakers: for the word *suit*, 47 per cent of people over 67 years old preferred the pronunciation *soot* (rhyming with *hoot*) rather than *syoot*. Among those aged under-28 the figure was 92 per cent, and much the same goes for *lute* and *enthusiasm*. Few people in Britain today would say *all-yude* for *allude*, and at least as many would say *sullooshun* as *sullyooshun* for *solution*. Older people in England still say *Tyoosday*, but among younger people, you are more likely to hear *Choosday*. Americans, falling between the two, tend to say *Toosday*. There was a similar result for the word *nephew*, which was almost universally pronounced *nev-yew* in the early 1900s: of the older age-group, 51 per cent preferred the pronunciation *neff-yew*, while among the under-28s, the figure rose to 92 per cent.

In the older group, 59 per cent preferred *appLICable* to *APPlicable*, compared with

91 per cent of the under-27s; *primARily* was preferred to *PRImarily* by 51 per cent of the oldest, but 77 per cent of the youngest. Possibly there is some American influence—*Webster's Dictionary* gives both pronunciations for *applicable*, but only the second-stress version of *primarily*—but searching for a reason for the change seems a futile occupation. The fact is that the survey gives a snapshot of a tiny part of the language as it will be in a few decades' time.

* * *

Anyone can hear that young people and old people speak differently. Of course the sounds of our speech alter as the muscles that produce them grow older—but the differences are more than simple physical changes. We carry the accents and pronunciations of our childhood with us through life—even people who work hard at changing their accents generally retain a few lingering traces of the way they spoke as children. In that very literal sense, old people speak in an old-fashioned way: their accents were fashioned a long time ago. Of course, the differences are sometimes camouflaged. There are young fogeys who affect the speech (not to mention the opinions) of old buffers, and older people who try to recapture their lost youth by talking like teenagers. Generally, it's done for much the same reason, and with the same degree of success, as middle-aged men who carefully train a few strands of hair over their balding pates. In short, it's not a good idea: a chimpanzee on a bike is still a chimpanzee, and an old person aping his children remains an old person.

The point is that we may try to stand still, but language doesn't. It always has changed, it is changing now, and one thing that is certain is that it will change in the future.

CHAPTER TEN

Four Fallacies and a Conclusion

Among many people, you can introduce the whiff of pomposity by talking about language, in much the same way as you can start a bad smell by stirring the mud at the bottom of a pond. The desire to lay down rules, to take the world back to a Golden Age of linguistic correctness, and at the same time to establish one's own credentials as an educated, sensitive soul is a temptation to anyone who even thinks about the way we speak.

But few people speak all the time as if they were reading the lesson in church—and speech, after all, is an immediate, almost instinctive, form of communication. It may be hard for a teacher to persuade her class that the vulgar *innit* is sloppy speech, but that *isn't it* is somehow more acceptable—especially when she has to admit that *is not it* would be downright stupid. There is a story of a Conservative backbench member of parliament, hearing a Labour colleague complain that he had 'an 'ell of an 'eadache,' suggesting that he should get a couple of aspirates—which he would have been expected to take, of course, only with with *'ell* and *'eadache*, and not with *'onesty, 'otels* or *'onoraria*. We speak as we please, and most people have command of several different styles of speech, to use on appropriate occasions. The writers of the BBC's pronunciation guide of 1928, *Broadcast English*, compared the distinction between everyday speech and formal language with that between the clothes we wear on different occasions. They observed that 'the kilt is as conspicuous in Piccadilly as the silk hat upon the moors'; accepting the fact that most of us in these less formal days are as little likely to wear a silk hat as we are a kilt, the same rule of thumb could apply today. By and large, any pronunciation that is easily understood and doesn't cause offence where none is intended is 'correct'.

So anyone who hoped for instructions from this book on how to lose an accent or 'speak properly' will by now have either tossed it aside or accepted that they are going to be disappointed. The only sensible rules on the pronunciation of English are those that native speakers follow automatically—that *g* is generally soft when followed by an *e*, for instance, or that doubling an *e* or an *o* lengthens the vowel sound, from *bet* to *beet* or from *cot* to *coot*. Similarly, a short *i* will usually be lengthened to *eye* by the addition of an *e* after a subsequent consonant, so that *pin* turns to *pine*. It's always easy, of course, to think of exceptions even to these basic rules. What about the hard *g*'s of *get together*, or the difference in pronunciation between *foot* and *boot*, and what about the *-ine* of *magazine*? But nobody gets those wrong. Similarly, few people would be able without thinking to draft a rule to explain how the sound of *s* and *z* makes the difference between nouns and verbs, but no one for whom English is their first language would fail to distinguish between the sounds of *to house* and *the house*, *to use* and *the use*, or *to excuse* and *the excuse*. Other distinctions, such as the one between the different *oo*'s of *foot* and *boot*, can't be explained logically, but are still almost invariably followed by people who have spoken the language all their lives.

Even when the rules reflect the way people speak, it is hard to find a reason for them. Two-syllable words that can be used both as nouns and verbs will generally have the emphasis on the first syllable when they're nouns, and on the second when they're verbs. It doesn't make any sense, but at first glance, it seems to work—*accent*, *confine*, *desert*, *export*, *present* and *subject* all follow the rule. But once again, for every rule that is laid down, anyone could find half a dozen exceptions by listening to half an hour's conversation in any pub or street corner—just try applying the rule to the words *rebuke* or *desire*. And when the rules deal with vowel sounds, they have to be interpreted particularly flexibly. A Yorkshire English speaker, for instance, may well pronounce *beetroot* as *baytroot*, and it would be inadvisable to correct him to his face.

Arguments over fashion are especially futile—the squabble over *skedule* or *schedule*, for instance, or *CONtroversy* or *conTROversy*. Those who think they are important should remember the passion with which Noah Webster defended the pronunciation *deef* instead of *deff*, or the magisterial authority with which the BBC's pronunciation guide of the 1920s ruled that the word *vitamin* should be pronounced *vyetamin*—one American pronunciation that has never caught on in British English. The word *tryst*, it said, should be pronounced with 'the vowel as in *rice*,' *culinary* should be pronounced *KEWlinary*, and *vagary*, vaGARy. The book was not produced by some group of old buffers, but by some of the finest linguistic minds of their day—the grandly-named Advisory Committee on Spoken English that was responsible for it included the Poet Laureate, Robert Bridges, and George Bernard Shaw. The point is that the task they were trying to do, taking a snapshot of a moving target, was an impossibility. Whatever rules they set out were bound to look archaic in a few years' time.

The BBC's Committee, being British, could not avoid bringing class into the matter—'A man's social class will be more evident from the fashion of his speech than from any other fashion he adopts,' the booklet said—but it was at least trying simply to lay down pronunciations that would cause the least offence to the least number of people. Other prescriptions can be more annoying: in discussing the word *harass*, one recent handbook of best practice declared prissily, 'Educated speakers of British English place the stress on the first syllable. Others do not.'[66] On the contrary, you could point out that there are no doubt Fellows of All Souls at Oxford and Nobel Prize winners who habitually say *harASS*, but the answer is even simpler. Why?

Often, those who claim to want to defend the language find themselves shouting in opposite directions at the same time. They complain that British English is being swamped by Americanisms, and then they grumble about dropped *h*'s and glottal stops—both of them habits which have never crossed the Atlantic. It's as well to remember the eighteenth-century London men of fashion who started to abandon the rhotic *r* in words like *farm* or *darling*. That change would certainly have been criticized in much the same terms as Estuary English is today—and yet without it, we would all be speaking like John Wayne. Yesterday's revolution is today's conformity.

The search for certainty and the aching desire to demonstrate superiority lead people into four separate fallacies when they start to pontificate about pronunciation. With similar

298

confidence, the same grammatical handbook that was so certain about the right way to pronounce *harass* turned to the word *schedule*: 'The British English pronunciation is, or used to be, *shedule*. There is no good reason to replace it with the American pronunciation *skedule*.' Except, of course, that increasing numbers of people do. This waving fist against the incoming tide provides a perfect introduction to the four great fallacies of pronunciation.

The Logical Fallacy
Whenever people look for a rational basis for pronunciation—for a 'good reason', as the grammatical handbook did—they end up by tying themselves in knots. At different times— and sometimes at the same time—the traffic wardens of language have sought to demonstrate that the rest of the world is wrong by pointing to spelling, to etymology and to analogy. Dr Johnson observed that the best speakers were those 'who deviate least from the written word . . .' but spelling, in a language that has been growing and developing for over a thousand years, is the most easily dismissed guide of the three. Modern spelling reflects attempts made several hundred years ago, using an arbitrary and insufficient collection of symbols, to reproduce the pronunciation of a particular

299

small group of people. It is hardly surprising that words like *ptarmigan*, *listen*, *pretty* and *knife* should sound so different from the way that they look.

George Bernard Shaw famously observed that the word *fish* could be spelled *ghoti*, by taking the *f*-sound of *cough*, the *i*-sound of *women* and the *sh* of *nation*. Some years later, he was outdone by a scholar who demonstrated that by taking the *phth* of *phthisic*, the *eigh* of *weigh*, the *ch* of *school*, the *ou* of *glamour*, and the *nd* of *handsome*, the word *taken* could just as convincingly be spelled *phtheighchound*. Anyone who still thinks that spelling is a good guide to pronunciation might consider the sentence, 'Some people coughed, although a pretty young woman was talking to two clerks and some friends.' Not great literature, perhaps, but a completely understandable sentence— every single word of which is spelled differently from the way it is pronounced.

Etymology is an even less certain guide. It may be interesting—indeed, it *is* interesting— to know that the word *knight* is derived from the Old English *knicht*, which was pronounced *k-nikh-t*, but it hardly increases our confidence in how to read the word today. One influential nineteenth-century guide to pronunciation complained that people had started to shorten the first syllable of the word *knowledge*, presumably by analogy with words like *shepherd* and *vineyard*, when the etymology of the word made it perfectly plain that it should be pronounced *noh-ledge*.67 It depends, of course, how far you take the etymology: the Old Norse *kna* or the Middle English *knaulage*, both pronounced with the initial *k*-sound, would suggest interesting pronunciations, but neither of them has much to do with modern usage.

So etymology, too, seems to fail us as a guide to pronunciation. But what about analogy? We are surely entitled to assume that a group of letters pronounced one way in one word will be pronounced the same way in another. My father, being a schoolmaster, was particularly exercised about issues like this, and one of the aspects of the war in the South Atlantic in the early 1980s that got under his skin was the way BBC newsreaders and journalists kept referring to the *Follklands*. He had reached that stage of late middle-age when all the rules he had grown up with were being challenged or—even worse—ignored: it was quite clear, he said, with perfect logic, that if *talk* was pronounced *tork* and *chalk* was pronounced *chork*, then *Falklands* should be pronounced *Forklands*. But of course, nobody listened. James Boswell said that Dr Johnson similarly insisted on making the word *heard* rhyme with *steered*, on the dubious grounds that to do anything else would make a single exception to the way in which the letters *ear*

301

were pronounced in English. One can only assume the great lexicographer had never heard anyone call him an old bear.

The Graphical Fallacy
The Reverend Archibald Henry Sayce was a Victorian Assyriologist at Oxford University and one of the leading authorities of his day on the language of the ancient Babylonians, on cuneiform writing, on hieroglyphics, and on the ancient history of the Middle East—but although he was so steeped in the study of antiquity, he was ahead of his time as a linguistic scholar. 'Language,' he said, in 1879, 'does not consist of letters, but of sounds.'**68**

In its time, it was a daring remark—linguistic scholars generally concentrated almost exclusively on the written word, and ignored spoken language. It's not hard to see why—as we have seen, it is difficult to establish how people spoke in the past, and written texts provide a straightforward and permanent subject for scholarly research. But Sayce was right in the sense that all languages either exist or have existed in a spoken form, while only a few have ever been written down. In historical terms, writing is very much the brash newcomer of language—while speech is estimated to go back more than 150,000 years, the earliest writing comes from barely 6,000 years ago.

The words written on the page, in fact, are the Johnny-come-Latelies, both literally and figuratively two-dimensional. We may say, sentimentally, that the poems of Shakespeare, of Keats, or of Chaucer speak to us down the centuries, but of course they don't. Words on the page are silent: they speak to us only in the same way that a picture on a television screen looks at us. They are not just the poor relations, but the arthritic, stumbling, inarticulate relations of speech. The differences between various accents fade into insignificance compared with the shared instinctive exactnesses of the way we speak. Compared with such subtleties, don't the grumbles over a few dropped *h*'s and elided vowels seem a bit petty?

Today, academics accept the differences and similarities between writing and speech—but the permanence and visibility of the written word mean that it is still often treated as if it were in some way a superior form of communication that speech should try and mimic. It is writing, in fact, that was designed to represent speech on the page, and not the other way round—but children today are still admonished, 'Don't drop your aitches,' or, 'Don't leave the *g* off -*ing*,' as if it were the written word that really counts.

That—the belief that pronunciation should as far as possible recreate the letters on the page—is the Graphical Fallacy.

The Golden Age Fallacy

By the time they reach middle-age, most people have discovered that everything used to be better once—and language is no different from anything else. 'During the reign of Queen Anne,' said the actor and elocutionist Thomas Sheridan in 1780, 'when English was spoken at Court . . . a gentleman or lady would have been as much ashamed of a wrong pronunciation then, as persons of a liberal education would now be of mis-spelling words.'**69** In fact, even though Sheridan cannot have had much more idea than we have now of how English was spoken in Queen Anne's day, sixty-five years before he was writing, he did have some cause for complaint. The succession of the German King George I marked the start of a period in which English was quite literally not spoken at Court. Under the Hanoverians, the King's English, in fact, was French. But the significant thing about Sheridan's complaint is that the death of Queen Anne came in 1714, just five years before his own birth, which is just about the favourite time to look back on nostalgically.

Elderly old buffers today reminisce fondly about a time before the pernicious influence of television, just as their parents looked back to the days when talking pictures had not begun to infect the speech of the nation's youth. Slightly younger old buffers may remember the golden days before home computers—and no doubt in a few years' time, people will be boring on about the dreadful influence of the iPod. It's worth noting in passing that when people complain about the decline of language, it is always other people's language to which they refer. But as they look backwards with regret, so they look forward with foreboding, just as Sheridan did: 'Now the greatest improprieties (of pronunciation) are to be found among people of fashion,' he moaned. 'Many pronunciations which thirty or forty years ago were confined to the vulgar are gradually gaining ground. And if something be not done to stop this growing evil and fix a general standard, English is likely to become a mere jargon which everyone may pronounce as he pleases.'

Which takes us neatly to the fourth fallacy.

The Apocalyptic Fallacy
There is not much fun in sighing for the past if you can't issue dire warnings about the future. That is what Sheridan was doing, and it is what people have done for generations about language. No less a voice than that of Robert Bridges, Poet Laureate in the early twentieth century, joined in. English, he said, was possibly 'on the road to ruin' because of the vulgar way in which unaccented vowels were being degraded by an uncaring populace.[70] It's a warning that can be found periodically in the

letters pages of otherwise serious newspapers: if people continue to say *bo'uw* instead of *bottle*, if they persist in saying *eh?* instead of *I beg your pardon*, if they don't use the subjunctive when they ought, sound their *h*'s or cross their *t*'s, or whatever vital aspect of communication has caught the attention of the writer, then the English language, the language of Shakespeare, as such correspondents are often keen to point out, will degenerate into a series of grunts.

Except, of course, that it won't. Languages change. It should be clear by now that the 'language of Shakespeare' already bears only the most tenuous relationship with the way we read the leaders in *The Times* or order drinks at the bar—although I have a friend who, being well-educated, 18, and very drunk, thought it would be amusing to order a beer in a Huddersfield pub called The Shakespeare Arms by speaking in blank verse. They threw him out into the street, and a good thing too. Spoken language, as we have seen, changes much more quickly than the written word, and the changes are seldom welcome to people who have spent their lives speaking in the old way—but languages do not simply wither away. They do die, but not like that. Sometimes, like Latin, they change so much that they are almost unrecognizable—Cicero or Julius Caesar would have a hard time following proceedings in the Italian

Parliament, or understanding the crowd watching Juventus play Roma—but there is no case in all the languages that are known to have vanished of one that sickened and died because people did not look after it, and were careless about how it was spoken. What happens when languages disappear is that, for various reasons, other ways of speaking become more popular and gradually take over until speaking Cornish, or Gaelic, or Jersey French is simply no longer an efficient way of communicating.

And those examples make the point: in terms of swamping and suffocating other languages, English is the aggressor, not the victim. It is risky to make confident predictions about language changes, but it seems fairly safe to say that the 600 million people who speak English today are not likely to stop. Whether it is a good thing or a bad, there will be more English speakers in 2050 than there are today, and almost certainly more still in 2100. The apocalypse is not on its way—and if it were, it would not be because of the way people treat their unaccented vowels.

And a conclusion . . .
The cheering conclusion is that we are better at language than anyone gives us credit for. All of us. If the traffic wardens slap a ticket on the way we speak, we should tear it up and throw

it, as politely as possible, in their faces. It's our language, not theirs. We are capable of following conventions in pronunciation, just as we are in grammar, that neither we nor most of the people who grumble could begin to explain. There may be rules that we are constantly nagged about, but we all follow linguistic conventions that are infinitely more complex without a thought. There may be arguments about *harass*, but the stresses in a sentence spoken by two native English speakers will generally fall around the same place. People who wouldn't recognize a 'form-word' if it jumped up and poked them in the eye will know not to emphasize words like *and, but* or *the* in a sentence; people who might have trouble explaining the difference between a verb and a noun will instinctively stress the second syllable of a verb like *desert*, and the first syllable of the same word when it is a noun. And not only do they know and follow those rules without a thought but, even more impressively, they also know when to break them. Any native speaker can gain a 'what's more' effect by stressing *and* in a sentence, despite the rule about form-words; people make the distinction between words like *desert* as a noun and as a verb, but they don't make the mistake of treating *desire* in the same way. They say *serene*, but they say *serenity*; they say *list*, but not *list-en*. Our grasp of language is phenomenal—and that applies to everybody, not just the grumblers and pedants who want to find fault with the way we speak.

It's more than just a mastery of the building blocks. We can change the way we speak to fit in with the situation we find ourselves in, or to fit in with the speech of the person we are talking to. Accents, like the weather, are always there, and anyone who claims to speak without one is talking nonsense, but *changing* an accent is something that most of us do all the time, and it is likely to become an even more common skill in the next few years.

There are dangers in this flexibility—one journalist, watching the Labour politician Denis Healey greeting boys in his Leeds constituency some years ago with a playful thump on the shoulder and a shout of 'Wotcha, lads!' observed sourly that he sounded as if he had learned his slang on a Berlitz language course—but most people have several different grades of speech into which they can slip without even noticing it. If the guy with the glottal stop looks as if he is going to get the girl, then the floppy-haired public schoolboy will rapidly learn to drop his expensive accent, however much his father has paid for it.

Long ago, young girls used to walk sedately up and down drawing-rooms with books on their heads to improve their deportment, and mouth, 'How now, brown cow' to purify their diphthongs. When I misbehaved as a small boy, my mother used to threaten to send me to the elocutionist—a cruel threat, but one that usually worked. Those days have gone—we live in a less formal, less deferential world, and our language is becoming less formal and less deferential to match it.

Language isn't black and white, like a book of rules, but a glorious spectrum of colour. And the truly wonderful thing about it is that it is alive. It is a garden, not a museum—words aren't stored in dusty cabinets, to be taken out and admired, but they grow, and change, and die, and are replaced by new ones. We may miss a few familiar old blooms or be grieved to see how they are slowly withering away, but there are always fresh shoots appearing if we choose to look for them.

And after all, however grave the sins of pronunciation of which we may be accused, nobody died. At least—remembering the tomatoes in the Lebanon civil wars—not usually.

NOTES

1 *Observer*, 13 March 1983, quoted in *Does Accent Matter?*, John Honey, Faber and Faber, 1989.
2 On Channel 4, 24 July 2005.
3 *Pygmalion*, 1912, Preface.
4 Michael Davie (ed.) *The Diaries of Evelyn Waugh*, 1976. Quoted in John Honey, *Does Accent Matter?*
5 Julian Critchley, *Westminster Blues*, London, Elm Tree Books, 1985. Quoted in John Honey, *Does Accent Matter?*
6 In his book *Outline of English Phonetics*, Berlin, BG Teubner, 1914.
7 *Keywords*, 1983.
8 *Clayhanger*.
9 Aleister Crowley, *Confessions*.
10 Anthony Powell, *Messengers of Day*, Vol. ii, p. 82.
11 To John Honey, who re-told the story in *Does Accent Matter?*
12 Quoted by John Honey, in *Does Accent Matter?*, 1989.
13 *Guardian*, 18 June 1999.
14 *The Centre of the Bed*, London, Hodder and Stoughton, 2003.
15 Alan Bennett, *Untold Stories*.
16 In his autobiography, *Broadcast Over Britain*, 1924.

17   In the foreword to the 1928 edition of the BBC's 'Recommendations to Announcers', *Broadcast English*.

18   Wilfred Pickles, *Between You and Me*, Werner Laurie, London, 1949.

19   *Writing Home*, p. xiii, Faber, London, 1994.

20   John Wells, for instance, in *Accents of English*, Vol. ii, Cambridge 1982. The descriptions of where northern *u*'s and *a*'s are found are largely taken from this book.

21   Gerry Knowles, *Scouse: a Lancashire Dialect with an Irish Accent*, Regional Bulletin, Lancaster University, 1977.

22   Dirk Robson, *Son of Bristol*, Bristol, Abson Books, 1971. Also quoted in Wells, *Accents of English*.

23   *Krek Waiter's Peak Pure Bristle*, by Dirk Robson.

24   Alan Bennett, *Untold Stories*.

25   On the British Library's *Voices of History*.

26   *A Child's Christmas in Wales* was recorded in 1952. It was first published in *Quite Early One Morning* in 1954, after Thomas's death.

27   Angus McIntosh, *An Introduction to a Survey of Scottish Dialects*, Nelson, 1952.

28   J. C. Wells, in *Accents of English*, goes into more detail about the Scottish *r*.

29   In a BBC Radio 4 interview in December 2003, for instance.

30 In *In Transit*, London, Macdonald, 1969.
31 John Honey, in *Does Accent Matter?*, London, Faber and Faber, 1989.
32 From *The Adventure of English*, Melvyn Bragg, London, Hodder and Stoughton, 2003.
33 This example from David Sutcliffe, *British Black English*, Oxford, Basil Blackwell, 1982.
34 Letter to John Waldo, 16 August 1813.
35 *Dissertations on the English Language*, 1789.
36 In *The Question of Our Speech*.
37 Quoted in the *Cambridge History of English and American Literature, 1907–1921*.
38 In *Domestic Manners of the Americans*, 1832.
39 Quoted in H. L. Mencken, *The American Language*, 1919.
40 In *I Lost My English Accent*, 1939.
41 Quoted by Dennis Adams and Hilary Barnwell in *The Gullah Dialect and Sea Island Culture* for Beaufort County Public Library at *www.co.beaufort.sc.us*
42 *Detroit News*, 17 December 2001.
43 *Washington Post*, 27 October 2005.
44 In *Narrative of a Voyage to New South Wales and Van Diemen's Land*.
45 Both these doctors are quoted in Sidney J. Baker's authoritative *The Australian Language*, 1945.

46 In *Australia Limited*.
47 *Fraffly Strine and Everything*, Ure Smith, Sydney and London, 1969.
48 In his book *Two Years in New South Wales*.
49 In his book *Gold Regions of Australia*, 1852.
50 In his book *The Australian at Home*.
51 The team was led by Professor A. G. Mitchell. Its findings are summarized by Arthur Delbridge in his article 'Standard Australian English' for *World Englishes*, 1999.
52 *More Please*, Viking, London, 1992.
53 *Etiquette in Society, in Business, in Politics, and at Home*, NY, Funk and Wagnall's, 1922.
54 Such as Donn Bayard of the University of Otago, writing in *Moderna Sprak*, 2000.
55 Quoted in *The Cambridge Encyclopaedia of Language*, David Crystal ed.
56 D. H. Lawrence, *Lady Chatterley's Lover*.
57 In *Modern English Grammar*, 1949.
58 In *The Innocents Abroad*, 1869.
59 *Don Juan*, Canto I, i, 39–40.
60 The term was first used by the linguistics lecturer David Rosewarne in an article in *The Times Educational Supplement* in 1984.
61 Paul Coggle, *Do You Speak Estuary?*, 1993.
62 Ibid.

63 Lloyd James, *The Broadcast Word*, London, Kegan Paul, 1935.

64 Rabbi Howard Cohen, in his *Introduction to the Hebrew Aleph Bet*, at www.sover.net/~bethelvt/alefbet

65 Professor J. C. Wells, for his *Longman Pronunciation Dictionary*.

66 *Between You and I*, by James Cochrane, Icon Books, Cambridge, 2003.

67 Smart's *Grammar of English Sounds*, 1812.

68 *The Science of Language*, Vol. ii, p. 339.

69 *General Dictionary of the English Language*, 1780.

70 Quoted in the *Cambridge History of English and American Literature, 1907–1921*.

BIBLIOGRAPHY

Andrew Taylor and HarperCollins*Publishers* would like to thank all those who have provided permission to reproduce copyright material.

While every effort has been made to trace the owners of copyright material reproduced herein, the publishers would like to apologize for any omissions and will be pleased to incorporate missing acknowledgements in any future correspondence.

Allsopp, Richard—*Dictionary of Caribbean English Usage* (Oxford University Press, 1996)

Bailey, R W and Gorlach, M eds—*English as a World Language* (University of Michigan Press, 1982)

Baker, Sidney J—*The Australian Language* (Sun Books, 1986)

Bakewell, Joan—*The Centre of the Bed* (Hodder and Stoughton, 2003)

Baugh, A C—*A History of the English Language* (Routledge and Keagan Paul, 1959)

BBC—*Recommendations to Announcers* (1928 edition)

Bennett, Alan—*Untold Stories* (Faber and

Faber, 2005)

Bennett, Alan—*Writing Home* (Faber and Faber, 1994)

Blake, N F—*Non-standard Language in English Literature* (Deutsch, 1981)

Bragg, Melvyn—*The Adventure of English* (Hodder and Stoughton, 2003)

Briscoe, Diana—*Wicked Scouse English* (Michael O'Mara, 2003)

Brook, G L—*Varieties of English* (Macmillan, 1973)

Brophy, Brigid—*In Transit* (Macdonald, 1969)

Cochrane, James—*Between You and I* (Icon Books, 2003)

Coggle, Paul—*Do You Speak Estuary?* (Bloomsbury, 1993)

Crystal, David ed—*Cambridge Encyclopaedia of Language* (Cambridge University Press, 1987)

Crystal, David—*Language and the Internet* (Cambridge University Press, 2001)

Crystal, David—*The Stories of English* (Allen Lane, 2004)

Dillard, J L—*Black English* (Random House, 1972)

Gimson, A C—*Gimson's Pronunciation of English*, revised by Alan Cruttenden (Arnold, 2001)

Gopalakrishnan, N N—*Indian English Phonology* (Prestige Books, 1996)

Holmberg, Börje—*On the Concept of Standard English and the History of Modern*

Pronunciation (Acta Universitaties Lundensis, 1964)

Honey, John—*Does Accent Matter?* (Faber and Faber, 1989)

Honey, John—*Language is Power* (Faber and Faber, 1997)

James, Henry—*The Question of Our Speech* (Houghton Mifflin Co., 1905)

Jones, Daniel—*Outline of English Phonetics*, 9th edition (Heffer, 1972)

Krapp, G P—*English Language in America* (Appleton Century Crofts, 1925)

Macintosh, Angus—*An Introduction to a Survey of Scottish Dialects* (Thomas Nelson, 1952)

McWhorter, J—*The Power of Babel* (Henry Holt, 2001)

Mencken, H L—*The American Language*, 3rd edition (Alfred A Knopf, 1963)

Mitchell, A G and Delbridge, A—*Pronunciation of English in Australia* (Angus and Robertson, 1946)

Mugglestone, Lynda—*Talking Proper*, 2nd edition, (Oxford University Press, 2003)

Orkin, M M—*Speaking Canadian English* (General Publishing Co., 1971)

Robson, Dirk—*Krek Waiter's Peak Pure Bristle* (Dervish Books, 1998)

Robson, L L—*Convict Settlers of Australia* (Melbourne University Press, 1994

Rowse, A L—*William Shakespeare, a Biography*, (Macmillan, 1963)

Strevens, P D—*Spoken Language* (Longmans, 1956)

Sutcliffe, David—*British Black English* Blackwell, Oxford, 1982)

Tauper, Abraham ed—*George Bernard Shaw on Language* (Philosophical Library, 1963)

Thompson, C V R—*I Lost My English Accent* (Nicholson and Watson, 1939)

Trudgill, Peter—*Sociolinguistic Variation and Change* (Edinburgh University Press, 2002)

Truss, Lynn—*Eats Shoots and Leaves* (Profile Books, 2003)

Wells, J C—*Accents of English* (Cambridge University Press, 1982)

Wells, J C ed—*Longman Pronunciation Dictionary*, 2nd edition (Longman, 2000)

Wells, J C—*Accents of English*, vols i,ii,iii (Cambridge University Press, 1982)

ACKNOWLEDGEMENTS

You can't study the way English is spoken just by reading books about it—and the people to whom I owe the biggest debt of gratitude never even knew how they were helping me. I'm thinking of the hundreds of men and women on the train home, or on the bus to work, or simply sitting in the pub, who must sometimes have noticed the oddball standing near them and obviously eavesdropping on their conversations, and never once called the police.

If I sound slightly disrespectful in the previous pages about the academic study of language, it's not because I don't realize what a debt I owe to the people who have written more learned books than I could ever have dreamed of. Chief among them is John Wells, Professor of Phonetics in the University of London, not just because of his books, his website—

http://www.phon.ucl.ac.uk/home/wells/

—or even his generosity in answering my questions, but because his writing and his enthusiasm originally stirred my interest in the whole subject of how we speak.

I've also had help from more friends than I can possibly list, among them Peter Carter, Elwyn and Caroline Evans, John Humphrys,

Tamsin Roberts and Mike Ward. In Yorkshire, my old friend and colleague Bob Cockroft, now Editor of the *Barnsley Chronicle*, had some good tales to tell and also put me in touch with Brian Sheridan, who probably knows more than anyone alive about the different accents of South Yorkshire; in Wales, Elsa Davies even tried valiantly but unsuccessfully to teach me Welsh; in Cornwall, Rod Lyon, a Cornish speaker and Grand Bard of Gorseth Kernow, finally overcame my scepticism about the prospects for the Cornish language; and from the US, Julian Bene sent a constant stream of ideas and stories.

Several people told me about their own experiences, including Joan Bakewell, Rory Bremner, Michael Cockerell, Dareus Howe, Sue Macgregor and Norman Rees, while Mandy Little, Monica Chakraverty and Jane Bennett gave me the benefit of their professional help and advice from start to finish. To all of them, my thanks.

My good friends Tony and Jean Conyers and Edna Organ must sometimes have wondered if they were ever going to get their books back—and on a slightly larger scale, the staff of the British Library and the London Library have been constantly helpful and co-operative.

John Miller and other members of Bosham Sailing Club were unfailingly patient with a man who couldn't tell a bowsprit from a boathook. I owe them more than a drink.

Penny Berry has shared in the whole book, as she shares everything. Telling the world the secret of how the French version of her name has plagued a succession of skiing holidays, as I do in Chapter Eight, may be a poor way of thanking her, but I hope she will forgive me.

And finally, as ever, my thanks go to Dr Tim Littlewood of the Haematology Department of Oxford's John Radcliffe Hospital, partly for his occasional demonstrations of finely-modulated Lancashire vowels, but more because without the skill and care of him and his National Health Service team, there would have been no book at all. They saved my life, and acknowledgements don't come much bigger than that.

Chivers Large Print Direct

If you have enjoyed this Large Print book and would like to build up your own collection of Large Print books and have them delivered direct to your door, please contact **Chivers Large Print Direct**.

Chivers Large Print Direct offers you a full service:

✧ **Created to support your local library**

✧ **Delivery direct to your door**

✧ **Easy-to-read type and attractively bound**

✧ **The very best authors**

✧ **Special low prices**

For further details either call Customer Services on 01225 443400 or write to us at

Chivers Large Print Direct
FREEPOST (BA 1686/1)
Bath
BA1 3QZ